How to Build and Operate a Sawmill

By Leonard L. Shertzer

President Chickasaw Lumber Co.,
Demopolis, Ala.

___

With Three Loose Charts of
Sawmill Lay-outs.

___

Reprinted from American Lumberman
Issues of March 18 — June 10, 1916.

___

Price, $1.00

___

American Lumberman

1918

FOREWORD.

It is not my purpose to write a prolix and technical treatise nor to act as advertising agent for any particular brand of machinery. That I write at all is because of my observation that many men who build sawmills do not know how to build them, either for efficiency or for economy, and certainly many men who operate them are squandering both their own and their country's resources.

I recently read in the AMERICAN LUMBERMAN a query as to whether there were any textbooks to be had on how to build and operate a sawmill. The answer was: "There is none." Prof. C. A. Schenck, formerly of the Biltmore Forest School, compiled a book on "Lumbering and Logging" to be used as a textbook in the school. It is a valuable work but it does not contain any practical suggestions that help the average sawmill man. It is too technical and anybody that knows the sawmill man knows he will not read a technical book. I do not assume fully to supply this need but simply to offer some practical suggestions, gleaned from experience and observation, that may help some others to avoid some of the mistakes I, myself, have made. I may also provoke some more competent authorities to take up the subject and to write something really worth while. Thus we would eventually build up some authoritative sawmilling literature. Nor do I assume to write for the man who owns his modern bandmill; makes more in a day than I do in a month, and knows the business better than I could ever hope to know it. He is too busy anyway to read what I have to say. He could probably write much better himself and say more in fewer words, but is too busy also for that. He will tell you he had to learn by hard knocks; let the other fellow do the same. Why should he give information gratis that cost him years to accumulate? I write rather with the man in view who operates the small sawmill, sawing anywhere from 10,000 to 30,000 feet a day, or the man who is contemplating taking a flyer in the sawmill business— the farmer who owns some timber and thinks he will turn it into lumber, having heard vague rumors of the high prices of lumber, and knowing what he has to pay for the few thousand feet he buys annually from the local lumber yard. There are also a large number of successful men who have made money in business or professions that are interested in timber as an investment. Later they decide, like the farmer, to manufacture their own stumpage. There are those also who have had northern sawmilling experience, and, having cut out, go south without taking time to study new conditions, thinking they know it all, enter into southern deals with northern experience. The pine operator saws hardwood and wonders why he does not make money out of it.

I have seen all of them come to grief and then accuse the whole lumber fraternity of being the biggest aggregation of scoundrels in any business of any kind, whereas it is but the operation of the law of compensation and they have but themselves alone to blame.

I want to try to show that to build and operate a sawmill is by no means a novice's job, and if I can help the novice to decide to stay out, or, if he has made up his mind to go in regardless and try it anyway, help him to get lined up right, I will in either case have accomplished some good.

L. L. SHERTZER.

CONTENTS.

How to Build and Operate a Sawmill.

CHAPTER I

TIMBER SUPPLY

The character and capacity of the sawmill should depend primarily on the character and amount of timber to be manufactured. I believe the cost of the mill should not exceed $1 a thousand on the available stumpage, and as much less as possible. In small tracts of a million feet or less a substantial portable mill is the most reasonable and most sensible. For one should bear in mind that when the timber is cut out, unless there is another tract to which to move, the mill is not worth 25 cents on the dollar for the actual cost of the machinery and the construction cost is a total loss. I think the prospective mill builder figures most safely when he counts each outlay as so much added to the cost of his stumpage. Thus: How much does my mill add to the cost per thousand of the stumpage I am to cut? How much does my railroad add? My logging equipment etc? Figuring in this way he will not build too far out of proportion if he knows stumpage values.

Frequently we see statements like this: "Three million feet of fine stumpage; as much more can be secured." The purchaser of this initial 3,000,000 should first be sure that the second 3,000,000 could be secured, or is actually secured, before he builds a mill counting on 6,000,000 feet. Six million feet of good stumpage would justify a very decent mill; 3,000,000 only a very modest one. The timber you have is all on which you should count in the erection of the mill, and then later on if you secure more you are simply that much better off, and are working out one or more small deals instead of a large one all at once.

There is considerable variation in ideas as to the quantity of timber in a tract, so that no guesswork should be taken as a basis on which to work, and an accurate estimate should be made by experienced and reliable cruisers to ascertain the quantity and kind of timber on a given tract. As a rule owners of timber think they have twice as much as they really possess. They will tell you a tree looks smaller standing than it does on the ground. The best timber and largest trees are a little farther over in the swamp, or beyond another hill where it is impossible to go today, and so on. Such explanations as these have misled many credulous buyers. A case recently came under my observation where an owner advertised 50,000,000 feet of virgin pine stumpage in one compact body. A prospective purchaser put a cruiser on it and he reported less than 15,000,000 feet of merchantable timber. No deal should be entered into without a dependable estimate of the timber being made. If the prospective operator is not an estimator he should, and can, easily secure competent service. There are responsible firms in the timber and estimating business that will cruise a tract and guarantee their estimate to saw out. Such a guaranty is a valuable paper to have on hand, as it helps one's credit to show it to the bank where money is borrowed in a small deal, and in a large one on a bond issue it is an essential.

When the location is on a river where the timber supply seems sufficient to last for many years, or on a railroad where logs can be secured on reasonable rates within a radius of a hundred miles, the size and cost of the mill can be proportioned to the financial and business ability of the owners. But many times have I seen mills out of all proportion to the timber supply of the owners and capital unnecessarily wasted in big mills that neither the timber supply nor logging capacity justified.

A large tract of timber in a compact body, say 25,000,000 feet or more, is worth more per thousand feet stumpage than the same quality of timber in a tract of 10,000,000 feet or less, and I would rather pay $3 a thousand stumpage for the former tract than $2.50 for the latter. For, aside from the fact that the larger tract would last longer and have that much more chance to appreciate in value, it is cheaper from an operating viewpoint. The larger the timber supply the more complete facilities one can put in for the utilization of waste that is, of necessity, lost in the smaller operation. Mistakes made in a larger deal have more stumpage value over which to be spread. A thousand-dollar error, or a thousand-dollar expense, in a 25,000,000-foot deal amounts to only 4 cents a thousand, whereas a five-hundred dollar error, or five-hundred dollar expense, in a 10,000,000-foot deal amounts to 5 cents a thousand. Half the expense amounts to more per thousand on the smaller deal. I cite this to show the man who owns the smaller tract that it is necessary for him to pursue a more conservative policy and practice a more rigid economy all through his operation than for the larger owner, because not only from the size of the deals but on the per thousand feet basis the smaller owner is at a disadvantage.

A Most Serious Mistake

One of the most serious mistakes many of the timber owners and operators make is to try to cut their timber up too fast. It is because of the present baneful get-rich-quick idea. Even as honesty is the best policy, so conservatism is the best policy. I believe we would all be better off in the lumber fraternity if we produced less with more quality—if we could or would work on the principle of "not how much but how well." The owner of 30,000,000 feet of stumpage would do better by himself, his family and his country by taking ten years to put it on the market instead of trying to put it on in five. The second half of his timber will have grown some in five years, and there will not only be more of it but, assuming that stumpage consistently increases in value, it would be worth more per thousand feet and the growth and increased value would more than pay for the interest on the investment. Moreover, assuming that experience counts for greater efficiency, the owner would conduct a more scientific operation the second five years than he did the first, producing his output more economically and getting more for it. This same principle goes further: If the man who owns the 30,000,000 feet of stumpage could be induced to manufacture it at the rate of 3,000,000 feet a year and handle it as suggested he could at all times keep his deal well within the bounds of his own personal control. He could manufacture as well as market his product with more care. He could save $1 a thousand average in the manufacture and get $1 a thousand more for his stock. This is not a theory but a demonstrable fact. But few men can resist the temptation to operate on a large scale as opportunities seem to open up to them. The result is that by the time they have received sufficient experience and hard knocks to teach them to do business right they have sawed out and must seek a new location, combating new conditions, and have made but half of what they should have made, if anything at all. Too much future good is sacrificed to a misconception of present need and an over-estimation of present ability.

Fifteen hundred feet of lumber at $20 a thousand is better than 2,000 feet at $15 a thousand. The money value, it is true, is the same but in the latter case it has taken one-third more timber to produce $30 in money value, and it has had to be logged, manufactured, carried and marketed. Yet nine average sawmill men out of ten are producing the 2,000 feet at $15. At the end of the day the question asked of the sawyer, the log scaler or the tallyman is, "How much did you cut?" and more thought is constantly devoted to increasing the cut than to getting a better grade out of the logs. The result is a constant over-production. I have seen so much of this and it is so general that I can not but dwell upon it at some length. The larger output not only has its baneful effect on the price and decreases the timber supply faster but it is harder and more expensive to shut down in case of a slump. The man who is producing to his limit has his credit strained in carrying a large stock; has an expensive logging force; has heavy payments maturing and says he can not shut down. He dumps stock at cost, and frequently less than cost, on an already glutted market in order to keep going, thus aggravating the condition and delaying improvement.

Those large firms that are producing and marketing hundreds of millions of feet annually are hurting themselves, the small operator and the country at large. Many of them realize it after the octopus is grown, but then they can not reduce his size. When the market is overstocked and the best judgment of the lumber world is to shut down they can not shut down. So they continue to run; decrease their timber supply, the most valuable asset they have, and the price of lumber keeps low, and the lumber is frequently manufactured at a loss on account of this continual over-production.

If the timber crop were like cotton or cereal that could be grown in a year it would matter little. But the trees we are cutting down have required from thirty to 100 years to mature. Some of them are 500 and 600 years of age. It is true there will be timber here when this generation is gone and I am not arguing for posterity, for mighty few of us are thinking of posterity, but for the stumpage owner's own good and for the good of this present generation conservatism is the best policy.

Speaking generally, the prevalent idea that timber is scarce and will soon be cut out is wrong. There will be timber here for our children, if not for our grandchildren, but I have tried to show that aside from public reasons it is to the sawmill man's own immediate interest to cut his timber carefully and with judgment; get the best grade possible out of the log and make 1,500 feet bring $30 instead of having to saw 2,000 feet to make the $30.

Consider your timber supply first. Build the mill in due proportion to the timber supply. Instead of taking one year to saw it all, take two and profit the second year by the experience of the first.

How many of us now wish we had the fine logs we sawed up a few years ago and got nothing for? It will be the same a few years hence when we look back on those we are sawing now.

CHAPTER II

LOGGING

It must be borne in mind that we are writing with the man in view who manufactures anywhere from 10,000 to 30,000 feet a day. We would like to reach the inexperienced man who is susceptible to advice, and to whom the simplest explanation is welcome. So many of us feel that all such articles as this are intended for the other fellow and there is nothing in them of value to us. There is always profit in the exchange of ideas and the man who in many respects might run a very slipshod business may have in one or two departments the most scientific management imaginable. Thus in the convention speeches and trade paper articles, out of much that is dross we might find some ideas that will many times pay us for the listening or reading.

It must be borne in mind also that it is impossible in articles of this kind to lay down fixed rules, applicable alike to all situations, because what is applicable in one situation is frequently impractical in another. One millman will show you where he does his steam skidding for $1.50 a thousand, while another figures he is getting off light at $2.50. One millman will feed his four-yoke ox team for $2 a day and keep them fat, while another, equally as successful, will show where his feed bill is $3 a day per team and can not be reduced without loss to his cattle.

The output of a mill is no greater than its logging capacity. The success or failure of a deal depends in a large measure on the methods and efficiency of the logging department. In discussing logging we will give average and authoritative figures on average conditions and endeavor to show what method of logging is best adapted to given conditions.

All logging operations are amplifications or modifications of one of four grand divisions as follows:

Steam skidding.
Pull boating.
Hauling with teams.
River logging, such as rafting, floating and driving.

The best method to be used depends upon physical conditions, upon the stand of timber per acre and the total quantity of timber to be cut. We will discuss in their order the various methods and the conditions under which the use of each is most advisable.

First determine how much timber there is to be logged. Then how much the stumpage can stand for investment in logging equipment. Then ascertain the cost of logging by various methods, and the machinery and equipment, or teams required.

When the quantity of timber justifies the building of a log road and the timber is in compact bodies a steam skidder is the most economical, but it must first be determined if the quantity of timber justifies a railroad and skidding machinery, for these things come high. Assuming that the conditions are right for a railroad and skidding we will see if it would pay to put in a railroad with the rolling stock and the necessary skidding machinery, counting on an average haul of three miles, in a tract of 10,000,000 feet of stumpage, assuming further that the operator has no other use for this machinery when he gets through with his present deal.

As a rule rail can be rented from the main line railroad at 6 percent a year on its second-hand value, which is cheaper than purchasing new rail and also better because a heavier rail can be secured than would ordinarily be purchased. I would not therefore advise the purchase of new rails for the log road unless they could not otherwise be secured. In counting the cost of the road we are not, therefore, counting the cost of the rail. The actual cost of constructing the road will vary from $1,500 to $5,000 a mile; $2,500 is probably an average, and we will figure three miles of road at $7,500. In the mountains it would cost more. In the level, dry, southern pine sections it will cost less. In swampy sections, or anything but dry, level ground, it will cost around an average of $2,500. We will therefore figure as follows:

Three miles of road at $2,500 a mile................$ 7,500
One logging locomotive............................ 5,000
Eight cars at $400 each........................... 3,200
One skidder, equipped with ropes and blocks........ 5,000

Total invested in railroad and equipment.......$20,700

This would mean an investment of $2 a thousand on the stumpage before starting to operate. Unless the stumpage was very valuable or had been secured for nothing it would not pay. This machinery depreciates at the rate of 10 percent a year and to get the actual cost per annum the interest on the investment should be figured and 10 percent charged off to depreciation each year, so the entire original cost would be charged off the books in ten years. By that time the machinery would either be worn out or would more than likely be replaced by improved machinery and methods and fit only for the scrap heap. If in the meantime the timber is cut out and an effort made to sell the equipment it will not realize much in proportion to its cost and is no asset to a deal that is closed down. I would not recommend such a logging equipment as the foregoing for less than 25,000,000 to 30,000,000 feet of stumpage.

The Proper Kind of Equipment

Where the timber grows thickly or is thick in sections it is sometimes advisable to bunch it with a skidder and then haul it with teams instead of building a railroad. This method can be applied to hilly and mountainous sections as well as sloughs. Use the skidder to bunch the timber and then haul it. For work of this kind the machine shown in figure 1 is applicable.

This is a light yet powerful logging machine that can be mounted either on wheels or a sled, so that it may pull itself through the woods by its own power, or be hauled along the road by a team. It is provided with two drums of suitable strength and gearing, and will handle any ordinary log. The pulling lines may be taken to the stumpage either by hand or animals, or a return line may be arranged. It will reach from 500 to 1,500 feet away from the machine and will clear up to forty acres at a setting. The approximate cost of such an equipment, complete with blocks and ropes, if mounted on a sled would be $3,000; with wheels and draft gear approximately $3,300. This machine can be operated by five or six men, depending on conditions. An equipment of this kind is especially recommended for small cypress and gum sloughs in the South, where the water often stands the year round and it is too boggy to haul direct from the stump. The machine can be set on the edges of the sloughs and all logs thus bunched on solid ground.

In all skidding operations the small end of the log should come first. The small end of the log should be slightly pointed, or rounded off, the more readily to pass obstructions. Where a horse can be used for the rehaul or a return line is used cones can be used similar to the illustration shown under pull boating, but for a small operation on a short haul they are not necessary. Figure 1 covers the actual skidding only. In case of a railroad operation where both skidding and loading are to be done the Clyde skidder and loader shown in figure 2 is applicable. This is the McGiffert loader equipped as a two-line skidder. It will bring the logs to the track from a distance of 800 feet on either side of the track. For this purpose a boom is guyed to stumps on both sides of the track.

This machine is self-propelling and it will be noted that the wheel frame can also be raised from the track

FIG. 1. SUGGESTED LOGGING MACHINE FOR THICK STANDS OF TIMBER

FIG. 2. CLYDE SKIDDER AND LOADER

thus permitting cars to pass it on one line. Where mill capacity will permit this machine can be used as engine, skidder and loader. The approximate cost of this machine is $5,000 to $7,000, depending on size and equipment.

A cheaper machine is made by the Clyde Iron Works, known as the Clyde ground skidder, shown in figure 3. The illustration shows the machine mounted on cars, but it is so constructed that it can be removed from the car and from the track, being mounted on steel side skids with a steel plate riveted to the bottom so as to form a proper base for sliding over the ground. This machine is a combination skidder and loader but, as will be noted, is not self-propelling. The approximate

cost of this outfit is $2,500 to $3,500, according to size and equipment desired.

A different style machine to do the same work is shown in figure 4. The loading is done by cables without a swinging boom. This is the Lidgerwood semi-portable ground skidder and loader. It consists of one double cylinder two-drum engine, and one double cylinder single-drum engine, with boiler and necessary blocks and rigging. It requires eight men to operate this machine where ground conditions permit the line to be returned by horse. Where it is returned by men it takes more men. The approximate cost of this equipment is $5,000.

For logging the larger cypress and tupelo swamps of the South a heavier equipment is required than that shown in the previous illustrations. In figure 5 are shown the machine and rigging applicable to heavy swamp timber. This is the Lidgerwood semi-portable skidder and loader. It consists of one double-cylinder three-drum engine and one double cylinder two-drum engine, with boiler and necessary blocks and rigging. It requires a crew of fourteen to operate and costs complete approximately $9,000. It will reach up to 1,000 feet from the track.

FIG. 3. CLYDE GROUND SKIDDER

FIG. 4. LIDGERWOOD SEMI-PORTABLE GROUND SKIDDER AND LOADER

The Pull-Boating System

For logging swamp lands along the banks of a river a system known as pull-boating is used. This consists of a double cylinder, double-drum engine placed on a barge. This is made fast to the opposite side of the river from that which is to be logged. Under favorable conditions it will reach a mile. The outfit complete with the necessary blocks and rigging, exclusive of the barge, costs approximately $7,000. The barge will cost $1,000 to $1,500, so a complete pull-boat will cost anywhere from $7,000 to $9,000. (See figure 6.) This method is used chiefly for timber that will float. Swamp oak and hickory are frequently logged with the cypress or pine and floated by being dogged between floating timber.

For logging in mountainous sections special machinery has now been constructed to meet the conditions, a type of which is shown in figure 6-A. This is the Clyde mountain skidder, which can be installed for from $3,000 to $5,000, according to equipment.

As timber increases in value and becomes scarcer, places that were formerly considered unprofitable or

FIG. 5. LIDGERWOOD SEMI-PORTABLE SKIDDER AND LOADER

FIG. 6. COMPLETE PULL-BOATING SYSTEM FOR LOGGING IN SWAMP LANDS

impossible to log will be worked, and the logging machinery companies are devoting special efforts to this
sort of equipment.

Steam Skidding the Cheapest

I have shown some of the best known and most widely
used types of skidding machinery with approximate
costs so that the prospective operator may form an
idea as to whether or not these methods are applicable
to his deal, comparing the cost of the equipment with
the deal to be operated. Steam skidding, where the
conditions are right, is the cheapest method of logging,
except one, which we will show later. But the cost of
the equipment, together with the volume of business that
must be done to make it pay and to make it the
cheapest method, is too large for the average operator.

FIG. 6-A. THE CLYDE MOUNTAIN SKIDDER

I would suggest to the prospective or inexperienced
operator that before deciding upon his method of logging he go to one or two firms of about the size that
his own deal will be, firms that he knows to be successful, and observe their methods. Get a place and
work in the department to be studied if necessary.
Then invite the representative of one of the first class
logging machinery manufacturers to come and go over
the ground. There are several high class firms of this
kind advertising regularly in the lumber journals. The
information they give is authoritative and they can not
afford to put their equipment into a location unsuitable
to its economical operation. As a case in point I know
of a prospective lumber manufacturer who did this.
The machinery representative came and, after a thorough survey of the proposition from a logging viewpoint, said: ''I have no equipment suitable for this
deal. You need to log this with teams.'' These firms
will also give all the necessary information about the
installation and proper operation of their machinery,
putting an expert on the ground to stay until the work
is running smoothly.

As this article is more in the line of practical talks
and suggestions than a technical treatise it might not
be inappropriate here to observe that sawmill men as a
rule do not seek nor accept much advice, either in their
logging department or any other; that is, it has not
been their practice hitherto. These conditions will
change now that it has become necessary to systematize
operations and to do business right in order to uphold
one's end. I believe the proportion of failures in the
lumber business caused by men thinking they know
when they do not know is greater than in any other.
It is a business calling for a great deal of technical
knowledge and experience and yet it seems to be the
lure of innumerable novices. It takes a lawyer to practice
law; a doctor to practice medicine; a furniture maker to
run a furniture factory and an architect and contractor
to construct a building; but anybody runs a sawmill.

In logging with teams two methods are to be considered: Oxen as against horses or mules. We have
tried to show that steam skidding is applicable to
densely standing timber; to mountainous sections, river
bottoms and sloughs, and to large deals. For scatter-

FIG. 7. EIGHT-WHEELED WAGON RECOMMENDED FOR WORK IN SWAMPS

ing timber and small deals teams must be considered. We will compare briefly the oxen, the horse and the mule. In the North and West horses are generally used; in the South and Southwest both oxen and mules. For short hauls, either in mountainous or swampy sections, I would recommend oxen. They will go where a horse or mule will not, and will walk and pull a load where the horse or mule will bog and balk. Oxen are generally worked in four-yoke teams. To feed a four-yoke team costs from $2 to $3 a day. When the mill is shut down they will keep in good condition grazing about eight months of the year, or they can be readily sold for beef. An ox will walk from thirteen to fifteen miles a day with a load. An authority declares that the ox produces only four-fifths the power of a horse of the same weight. But

An eight-wheel wagon is recommended for swampy work where plenty of wheel base is required and is especially adapted to oxen. The wagon shown in figure 7 is a fair type of this wagon. It costs from $125 to $150, according to accessories.

For long hauls and solid roads, the four-wheeled wagon, being lighter, is better. That shown in figure 8 costs $80 to $100, according to width of tire and weight.

For skidding logs about the mill, miscellaneous work and punching, a bummer or go-devil is recommended, a low two-wheeled vehicle as shown in figure 10. The method of loading is shown in figure 9. The cost ranges from $30 to $35.

For hauling long logs and to get into difficult places where it is hard to go with the wagon, as well as for regular logging work, the old high wheeled logging cart is worthy of consideration, and has its place in the

Pat Sep 18 1900
May 14 1902
In Position to Load—

Half Loaded

Loaded

FIG. 9. METHOD OF LOADING

there is only about one-third the investment in the ox, and it costs less to maintain him. Horses and mules are generally worked in teams of four. For long hauls on solid ground I would recommend horses or mules. They will walk from twenty to twenty-five miles a day with a load, according to conditions. The investment is greater than in oxen and the animals require more care. The depreciation is greater in proportion to the investment and the cost of maintenance is greater in a shut-down. Scientific data and information as to feeding can be obtained from the secretary of the Southern Logging Association, New Orleans, La., a valuable association for the promotion of better logging methods, more standardization, and greater efficiency in all departments of the logging business.

FIG. 8. FOUR-WHEELED WAGON RECOMMENDED FOR LONG HAULS AND SOLID ROADS

catalog of logging machinery. Carts cost from $75 to $100. (See figure 11.)

I stated there was one method of logging cheaper than steam skidding, but it is limited geographically and restricted to floating timber. In sections of the South along the rivers the hardwood swamps are subject to several feet overflow nearly every spring. The trees are girdled in the fall, that is, cut all the way around through the sap. This is called deadening, as the sap runs out and the tree dies. Float roads are prepared, and when the rains begin in January or later the trees are felled and prepared for floating as soon as the water backs up over the swamps. When the water rises they are floated out to deep water, rafted and run to the mill. Thus timber that would be very expensive to log is made very reasonable by taking advantage of the overflow. The one great risk about this method is that there are seasons when the water does not come. Then the operator must endeavor either to

FIG. 10. BUMMER OR GO-DEVIL RECOMMENDED FOR MISCELLANEOUS WORK

get his timber by teams or by skidding, or it will be very seriously damaged before another season.

It might be well here to state that practically all the pines or coniferous trees will float green from the stump. Cottonwood, chestnut, ash, basswood, poplar and certain species of tupelo will do the same. Cypress, tupelo and gum should be deadened. Gum will not all float by deadening and in order that it may carry safely it should be peeled and allowed to stand a week or more. Oak, hickory, beech, birch—in fact, any wood that weighs four pounds or more dry to the board foot will not float.

There are other methods of transporting logs to the mill such as flumes and slides in the mountains and loose drives in the rivers, applicable to local conditions and which have to be decided upon by the operator.

The work to be considered in the woods is as follows:

Character or grade of tree to be cut.
Minimum diameter to be cut.
Proper felling methods.
Proper log lengths.
Cutting the tree into log lengths to best advantage.

Work to Be Considered

THE TREE TO BE CUT. Not enough attention is paid by the average millman to the tree that he cuts. A number of firms, especially pine operators, clean the ground as they go, cutting everything that will make one 2 x 4. This might do for a pulp manufacturer but not for a lumber manufacturer. I think 8 inches at the small end for pine and 12 inches for hardwood is the minimum that is profitable, and I do not recommend cutting smaller sizes. Nor does it pay to cut a poor log that makes all No. 2 and No. 3 common lumber, just because it is on the land and the stumpage may have been paid on it. Of course, if it can be shown that No. 2 and No. 3 common can be manufactured at a profit it is all right to saw low grade logs, but mighty few operators have ever been able to figure that, and if they have they have generally fooled themselves.

The first requisite to good lumber is good logs, and the very finest organization can not make high grade lumber out of poor logs. The way to make money out of poor logs is to leave them in the woods. If the timber is suitable for ties and a satisfactory tie order can be obtained, or a sound and square edge order that will net some profit, it is all right to saw low grade logs but to put them into lumber is wrong if dividends are a consideration.

PROPER FELLING METHODS. A great deal of waste is made by cutting too high from the ground. The best timber is in the butt cut and a foot or more of this is frequently left on the stump that should go to the mill. Unless trees are swell butted have them cut 6 to 8 inches from the ground. Sawyers will not cut low

stumps unless ordered specifically to do so and it is necessary for the management to look after this matter. This is also true of the selection of the trees and the proper cutting into log lengths. The men who do the actual sawing in the woods have more brawn than they have brain and their work must be mapped out for them, minutely and specifically, if they are to obtain the best results. And for the management of a sawmill operation to make money, that being the ultimate end for which they are in business, they must begin at the stump. One baneful condition in so many of our sawmill operations is that the concerns are there only for what they can get out of it. They desire to get what they can and get away. Hence there is no thought of conservation for a second cut, nor of the necessity of the close utilization of timber.

PROPER LOG LENGTHS. In ordinary hardwood and yellow pine shed stocks logs should be cut about one-third each 12, 14, and 16 feet long. Cut 3 to 4 inches over length in each case to allow for equalizing. Shorter lengths are made in trimming. In the Appalachian districts operators have been sawing too many 12-foot lengths and consequently consumers are kicking about the large percentage of 12-foot stock. At a recent meeting of yard men and consumers it was decided that they would insist upon at least one-half 14- and 16-foot stock in future shipments. In order to secure

FIG. 11. HIGH-WHEELED LOGGING CART FOR DIFFICULT PLACES

one-half or more 14- and 16-foot stock it is necessary to saw two-thirds the logs those lengths because the percentage will be reduced by trimming. The tendency to saw shorter logs is caused by a lower grade of timber. It will be seen that in a 16-foot board there is one-third more board to contain defects than there is in a 12-foot board, and the inference is that a higher average grade is obtained in shorter stock. But over against this the 16-foot log can be handled all the way through the operation about as fast as a 12-foot and any loss in the grade is about offset by the gain in handling. Moreover when it comes to selling the stock, the percentage of 14- and 16-foot demanded necessitates that it be cut, and it will command a readier sale. Cypress should be cut into log lengths of about equal proportions 10 to 20 feet; dimension stock and timbers, of course, to suit orders and demand.

For skidding and handling medium sized logs, even with teams, it is more economical to haul the whole tree. It is much easier to skid trees than short logs as they do not tangle up. More timber is being handled by the same amount of work as it requires fewer trips to carry the same amount of logs, and as a rule more attention is given at the mill to sawing proper log lengths than in the woods.

CUTTING THE TREE INTO LOG LENGTHS TO BEST ADVANTAGE. This is a matter requiring more study and attention on the part of the management than it usually gets. The matter of the close utilization of timber with ample space given to proper cutting into log lengths has been covered very competently by Prof. Ralph C. Bryant, of the Yale Forest School, in an address before the Southern Logging Association, at its convention in New Orleans, La., September 23-25, 1912. [This address appeared in full in the September 28, 1912, issue of the AMERICAN LUMBERMAN.]

A Few General Observations on Logging

To sum up a few general observations on logging I submit the following:

Logging is the hardest physical work connected with an operation. The wear and tear on men, machinery and cattle is the greatest. The leaks, the waste and consequent losses in this department will be in proportion unless they are closely watched and scientifically managed. The success or failure of a deal begins at the stump. High grade logs sent to the mill will produce high grade lumber. Sorry logs will produce sorry lumber.

One can not tell what his logging is costing unless he has some sort of a cost system. The average small operator is weak on this score. He has no accurate cost system, if any at all, and then begins to lock the stable after the horse is gone. The bookkeeping should also begin at the stump and the cost of each operation checked up as follows:

Sawing—actual felling and cutting into lengths.

Skidding—if any to higher ground, to track or bunching.

Swamping—time, if any, in clearing roads etc.

Hauling—transportation by whatever method.

Stumpage—stumpage value added to actual logging and transportation expense.

Depreciation—add to above the average daily depreciation figured at 10 percent per annum and interest at 6 percent per annum, or 16 percent per annum on teams and equipment and it will give the cost of logs at the mill by dividing the total by the quantity of logs hauled that day.

CHAPTER III

BUILDING THE MILL

I have stated in a previous chapter that a good plan to follow is that the cost of the mill should not exceed a total of $1 a thousand on the stumpage in sight. For 5,000,000 feet build a mill costing not to exceed $5,000. For 10,000,000 it could cost more, but it would be the policy of wisdom to keep it also around $5,000, remembering that a sawmill is simply a means to an end. As an investment it is not worth 25 cents on the dollar, hence the more there is invested in the mill the more the deal will have to make to uphold the proper proportion of profit. By this I do not mean that the mill building should be cheaply constructed, nor that the machinery should be light or cheap machinery, but simply that a sense of proportion should be maintained.

We all know of instances where mills have been built out of all proportion to the financial strength of the firm as well as the timber behind it. The result is failure. The plant is carried on the books as an asset of $50,000 and in the wind-up of the firm's affairs it is sold by the receiver for $10,000 or $15,000. I know of a case in point worse than that: One firm bought a few acres of ground as a site and built a river mill. The ground and mill cost approximately $75,000. The concern went in deeper than it expected and had to borrow before it was through. The panic of 1908 hit it with its money all tied up in a plant and with maturing obligations staring the concern in the face. It was forced into bankruptcy and a successful firm bought the whole deal, land and all, for $10,000.

For small tracts of timber ranging from 1,000,000 to 5,000,000 feet I would recommend a good substantial portable mill. Portable mills can be had from $1,500 to $3,000 in proportion to weight and equipment. I would in all instances recommend a three-block carriage, a three-saw edger and a two-saw trimmer. Some small operators try to run with a two-block carriage, a two-saw edger and no trimmer at all. It is a mistake, whether sawing pine or hardwoods. Having machinery too light, or not enough of it to make lumber is not the kind of economy I am trying to preach.

Figure 12 shows an average portable carriage and husk. This is the Cliff Williams No. 5 mill used for both pine and hardwood. It can be furnished with friction or belt feed, and with engine and boiler power ranging from 40 to 70 horse as desired. In all operations whether portable or stationary I would recommend getting plenty of boiler and engine power, because a mill is always added to and very seldom taken from. Thus if 50 horsepower will run the machinery you originally installed, get a 70 horsepower boiler and engine so when you add one more machine you are not handicapped for steam and power. This mill, with about 70 horsepower behind it, a heavy three-saw edger that will run three saws at once through a 2-inch board, and a two-saw trimmer, will make good lumber.

Another kind of a portable mill for sawing ties and lumber is shown in figure 13.

This mill is made in four sizes by the Salem Iron Works, Winston-Salem, N. C., and is suitable for both ties and lumber. It will turn out from 450 to 500 ties a day, besides the siding lumber, or will produce from 8,000 to 12,000 feet of boards, according to logs and general conditions. A mill of this kind can be moved and started in a new location in half a day. In purchasing and operating portable machinery the proper regulation of speed, size of pulleys in their relation one to another etc., are adjusted by the manufacturers and they will send a competent man to start the machinery properly at the first stand. In building a portable therefore it is not necessary to have a millwright, as it is more a matter of "setting-up" than it is of building.

In addition to the manufacturers previously mentioned the following also make portable sawmills: The Lane Manufacturing Company, of Montpelier, Vt.; the Ameri-

FIG. 12. CLIFF-WILLIAMS No. 5 MILL USED FOR BOTH PINE AND HARDWOODS

can Sawmill Machinery Company, of Hackettstown, N. J. (see figure 18); and the Portable Band Sawmill (Inc.), of New York City.

For portables and small circular mills where an experienced filer can not be employed profitably inserted tooth saws are best. The original cost of the inserted tooth saw is greater than the solid but it is easier to maintain, and will last longer than the solid saw and is the best saw for the small deal.

Competent Millwright Necessary

For building a stationary mill, anything larger than a portable, I would insist upon a competent millwright doing the work. The operator makes a serious mistake in attempting to build his own mill unless he is a competent millwright and knows thoroughly what he is doing. The trouble is that so many men think they know when they do not know. They are the hardest kind to tell anything. They think they are better millwrights than they are, just as they think they are better sawmill men than they are. The reason so many plants cost twice as much as they were originally estimated to cost is because proper and authoritative estimates were not originally made and the added cost is caused by blunders, changes and the inability to tell beforehand how much timber will be needed and how many men will be required a given time to do the work. When the plant is finished on time or within the allotted estimate it is the exception. Most frequently something is wrong, and much time and good money are spent in changes and corrections. One pulley is too large, another too small. The speed of one is wrong, the saw runs too fast, or a

room, one sawdust conveyor and one refuse conveyor to burner. Allow space for a nigger so that if necessary it may be put in later. Figure on a single 6- or 7-foot band of moderate speed to cut, say, 20,000 feet a day and to cost $10,000. He would then draw off a floor plan something like that shown in figure 14.

This is the typical floor plan of the average mill. I would suggest plenty of space on the mill floor. For example, leave space between the back of the bandmill and the front edger table to pile boards in case the edgerman gets behind in his work. Also leave space out beyond the trimmer, in both the width and length of the mill, so that later if it is decided to install more machines for the utilization of waste there would be ample room. The filing room can be built either at the side or on top of the mill. I prefer the top of the mill for greater convenience in changing saws, as the saw can then be let down into position by a tackle from above and pulled up the same way, more readily than it can be handled on the mill floor. For the filing room to be built overhead requires a solid mill building, or the filing room can be supported on timbers independent of the main framework to avoid excessive vibration.

There should be as few machines in the mill as possible to do the work desired. The more machinery there is—conveyors, chains etc.—the more there is to get out of order and to need repairs and supplies. And these accessories are what run up the cost of the plant.

I would recommend two engines, one to run the main saw, the haul-up and the sawdust conveyor, the other to run all machines in the back end of the mill. This will

FIG. 13. SALEM IRON WORKS PORTABLE MILL FOR SAWING TIES AND LUMBER

shaft is out of line and runs all the boxes hot. All of this can be avoided by employing in the first place a competent and reliable millwright—one known to give satisfactory results. If he is not known to you personally but simply comes to you well recommended let him tell you of some of the mills he has built and if possible you ought to go to see one or two of them. See how they run. Find out how the management is pleased with them. See if the minimum number of men are employed and the lumber progresses through the mill with ease.

Having secured the millwright, tell him just what is wanted and what you wish to invest in a mill, independent of kilns or planing mill. Say that the mill consists of a chain haul-up, bandsaw, carriage overhead turner, twin engine feed, edger, trimmer, cut-off saw and one bolter and dimension, or lath or shingle mill, filing

permit one end of the mill to run without the other. For example, suppose the edger and trimmer get behind. They can remain in operation and catch up some while saws are being changed, or the lath and dimension mill can run without using the big engine. Two engines will also avoid the use of a gear, which is expensive, subject to getting out of order, and makes lots of noise. Or where two engines are considered too expensive or too much machinery a tightener can be arranged on the main saw belt that can be raised to allow the main saw to stop while the back end of the mill is running.

I would in all cases recommend some machinery for the utilization of waste; in wood suitable for shingles and lath, such as pine, cypress and fir, both a lath and shingle mill; in oak and gum, a dimension mill to make chair stock and miscellaneous small dimension.

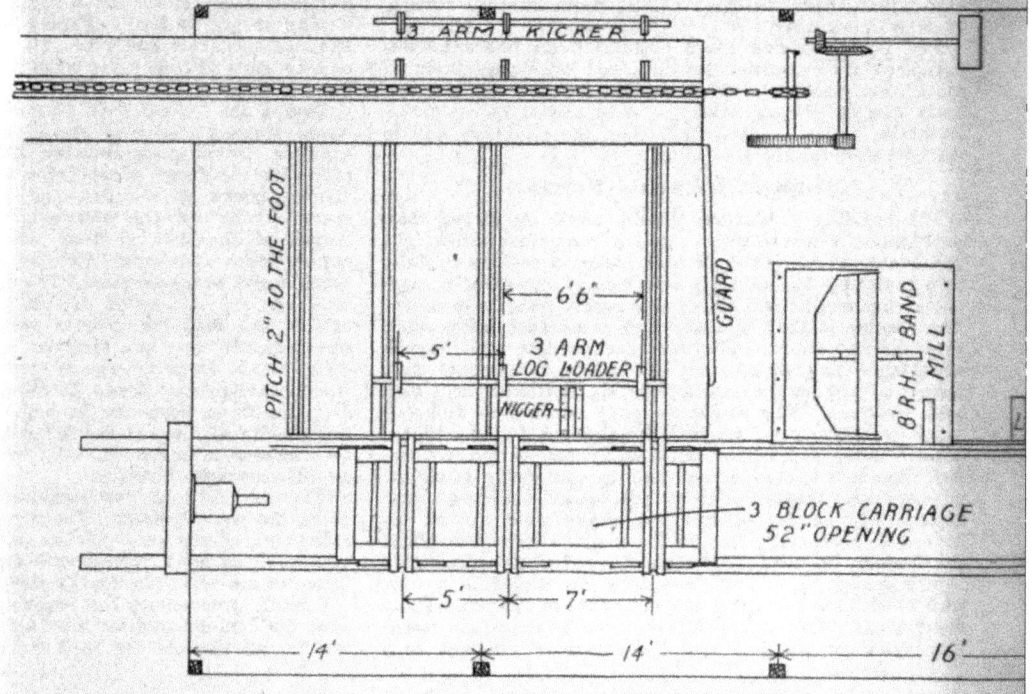

FIG. 14. FLOOR PLAN FOR SUGGESTED MILL, WITH PLE[N...]

Dimension stock brings about the same price as No. 1 common and can be made from stock much of which would go to waste without the machinery to utilize the small dimension. Machines to utilize stock that will not go into lumber, if properly handled, will pay the mill's pay-roll. Factories would rather buy the sizes they use cut to exactly what they want than to buy the lumber and have to cut it up; so they are always ready, under normal conditions, to place orders for the sizes they require in small dimensions in such woods as oak, ash, gum and hickory. Special sizes for crating lumber to be made from any kind of sound lumber are also in demand. Therefore, in building the mill provision should be made for this class of work, and if the machinery is not installed at the time the mill is built there is wisdom in arranging for sufficient space on the main floor for installation of such machinery as desired.

Just what is required should be explained fully to the millwright before he starts. He will then cover the various items in making his plans and can tell, if he is a competent man, within $500 of what it will cost to build the mill desired. Thus, given the cost of the machinery, the cost of the mill can be made what the builder desires, and for a mill to cost more than it was at first intended or enough more to hamper the finances of the builders is due more to incompetence and carelessness in making estimates and plans for the work than it is to necessity.

Economical Handling of Lumber Should Be Aim

The economical handling of the lumber to obtain the results desired should be the constant aim of the sawmill operator. Frequently much useless labor is employed in getting the lumber from the mill to the kiln or yard, and from the kiln to the planers. Much of this can be avoided by grading the lumber right at the chains as it comes off the trimmer. Have two long conveyor chains, 50 to 100 feet, run out from the trimmer at a slow speed, the length of the conveyor to be determined of course by the conditions. Let the mill inspector tally and put a grade mark on the stock as it passes along this conveyor and then it can be separated on buggies or kiln trucks as desired. It costs less to separate the grades before the stock goes to the yard or kiln or in the process of going than it does afterwards, and as the separation is eventually necessary it should certainly be done first in order to have a record of what is being done. In the very beginning of the operation, that is, in the building of the mill, provision should be made for this work, as its importance can not too long be dwelt upon. It is here that the small mills fall down. They do not inspect their stock as it comes through the mill. It is sent to the yard or kiln, and is frequently sold log run. They consequently get about half of what it is worth and then wonder why they can not make money in the sawmill business. An inspector at the tail end of the mill is just as essential to the operation of a well regulated plant as a sawyer or edgerman. He need not be an expensive man. An intelligent laborer or a young man starting in can soon be educated to do this work in a satisfactory manner.

In addition to separating the grades the lengths should be separated, and for convenience and economy in this work an automatic length separator can be built in even the smallest mill with very little expense, as shown in figure 16.

It is always well to bear in mind in starting to build that the plant will probably be enlarged by the addition of a conveyor here or an extra machine there, thus requiring more power. This should be anticipated and sufficient boiler and engine power installed to run a plant about half again as large as the one started. For a mill such as that shown in figure 14, a medium single band, a boiler about 72"x18' would run it all right, but two boilers slightly smaller, with a little more combined horsepower than the one large boiler would be better. To get efficiency out of boilers they must be kept clean, and the furnaces kept tight. The management is usually lax along these lines, leaving this class of work to watchmen and firemen without supervision, and much time is lost for lack of steam that could readily be avoided by proper

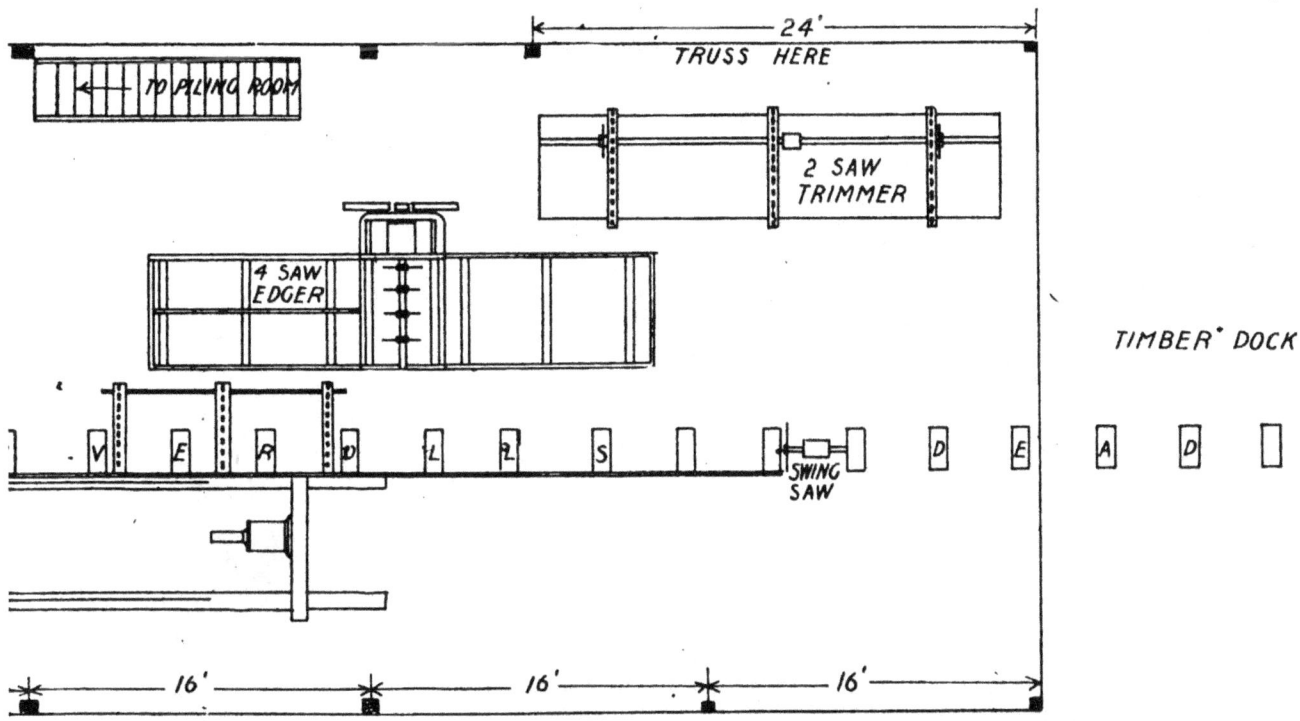

F WORKING ROOM AND SPACE PROVIDED FOR FUTURE ADDITIONS TO EQUIPMENT

attention to the boilers and furnaces. For burning saw-dust and green fuel a dutch oven is recommended, a simple illustration being shown in figure 17a. This is a patented oven manufactured by Quinn & Co., of Cincinnati, Ohio. An oven of this kind can be installed for a reasonable cost and will save many fuel troubles. The Casey &

FIG. 15. GORDON HOLLOW BLAST GRATE FOR UTILIZING GREEN FUEL AND SAWDUST

Hedges Company, of Chattanooga, Tenn., also manufactures a dutch oven suitable for the purposes above mentioned.

Where the cost of a dutch oven is considered too much or is disliked for any reason the Gordon Hollow Blast grate manufactured by the Gordon Hollow Blast Grate Company, of Greenville, Mich., is very effective in making steam out of green fuel and sawdust. This is illustrated in figure 15, and where it has not been built with the furnace it can later be installed in most any ordinary furnace. Another satisfactory grate is the "Improved Hot Blast Grate" manufactured by the Hot Blast Grate Company, of Traverse City, Mich.

One or the other of these appliances is urged, especially in hardwood mills where it is desired to burn the sawdust or where the fuel is not only green but wet from river or pond logs, because lost time from lack of steam soon runs into money with all the mill crew idle. The boiler power does not help unless the steam is kept up, and these are the most effective means to keep it up.

Utilization of Sawdust.

There has been a good deal of discussion about the utilization of sawdust. As a rule the best way to use it is to burn it in the furnaces or send it to the burner when there is too much for the furnaces. It depends upon the location of the mill whether or not any of the sawdust can be used for other purposes. The following is quoted from an article published in the AMERICAN LUMBERMAN some time ago in answer to an inquiry as to the best methods of disposing of sawdust:

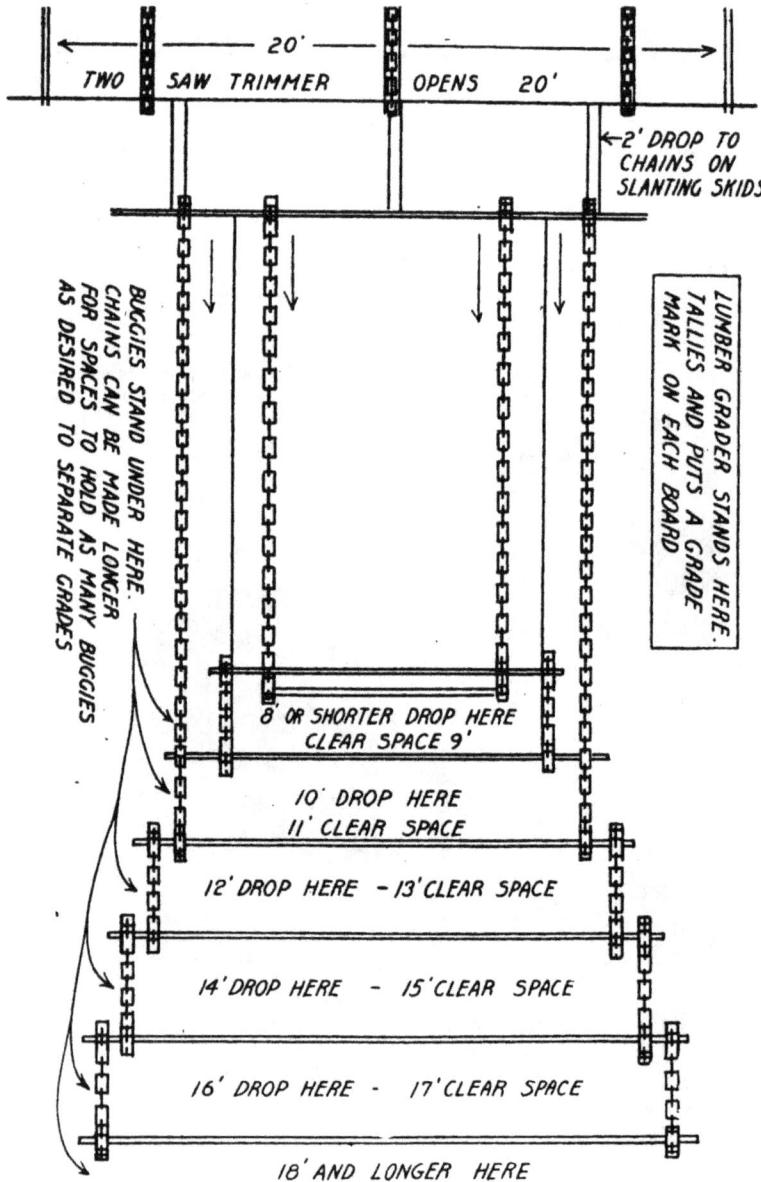

FIG. 17. McDONOUGH DOG

The profitable utilization of sawdust is a problem which thus far has been solved satisfactorily only in close proximity to large cities. In Chicago there is at least one firm whose business is exclusively confined to the distribution of sawdust which is used for bedding, for packing and for sprinkling floors in saloons etc. There are only one or two locations in the United States where sawdust briquetting has proved profitable and these have been where there is a large local population to consume the fuel, saving long distance transportation charges.

There are numerous other uses for sawdust which require great detail in specialization in order to arrive at success. Hardwood sawdust is successfully used for the

FIG. 16. AUTOMATIC LENGTH SEPARATOR

FIG. 17a. DUTCH OVEN OF THE
QUINN & CO. MAKE

manufacture of oxalic acid. It is stated that by a German process sawdust is digested with sulphuric acid and converted into a product containing approximately 25 percent sugar and the remainder soluble and insoluble carbohydrates. A stock feed is then elaborated with incidental by-products. Such a process is, of course, out of the question for the ordinary sawmill or lumber plant. The sweeping compound which is sold at the grocery at 10 cents a pound or three pounds for a quarter has sawdust as its base, incorporated with other substances. In the coarser of these compounds the sawdust is used in its original form while in other instances it is reground into a coarse wood flour. The finer grades of wood flour are used in the manufacture of gunpowder, linoleum and for other purposes, but are imported from abroad at a price which does not leave much room for profit for manufacture in this country.

FIG 18.
KNIGHT DOG

Oak sawdust is used by the packing houses for curing their meats and where the rates are permissible there is an occasional outlet for a car of oak sawdust through this channel at a nominal price, but any price is profit. It pays, however, as far as possible to burn the sawdust in the furnaces, thus turning it into steam and saving the wood for sale, for in many places there is demand for wood where there is none whatsoever for sawdust.

This is where a bandmill has the advantage over the circular. It not only makes more lumber but there is less sawdust to be disposed of. The ordinary circular saw will take out a kerf of one-fourth of an inch, while the band will make a kerf of one-eighth to three-sixteenths, or about half that of the circular. Besides the advantage of having band-sawn lumber the band will produce from 50,000 to 75,000 feet more lumber out of a million feet of logs than the circular. The band mill, of course, costs a little more to maintain but in the course of sawing 10,000,000 to 15,000,000 feet it will pay for itself and be clean profit over the circular mill.

A number of mills, especially circulars, have a practice of making the last board in the log, or dog board, 6/4 or sometimes 8/4, when all of the remainder of their cut is 1-inch stock. This is very unnecessary and in the end very costly because in many woods there is no demand for the backing boards, which are practically all Nos. 2 and 3 common in this thickness. For example, in gum where the Nos. 2 and 3 common grades are used chiefly by the box factories they do not want 2-inch stock at all because they have to resaw it and it does not work

to the thickness desired like 4, 5 or 6/4 stock. Unless sawn for some special purpose where 2-inch is desired the backing board need not be over the thickness of the other stock that is being sawn, 4, 5 or 6/4 as the case may be. By the use of the McDonough dog, figure 17, the last board can be sawed 1 inch and if the carriage is true the board will be all right. This is manufactured by the McDonough Manufacturing Company, of Eau Claire, Wis.

It is strange how firms will run on indefinitely doing a thing wrong because it has been done that way, and many times thousands of dollars will be lost in making the lumber wrong when a slight improvement or change that can be made in a half day would remedy the whole matter. This matter of sawing mis-cut and thick backing boards has cost many firms more on every day's cut than the cost of the improvements that would be required to make the last board as perfect for manufacture as the first, and yet they run on either through carelessness or ignorance until they have a great pile of backing boards on the yard that must be sacrificed to be moved at all.

For quartersawing the special Knight dog (see figure 18) manufactured by the Knight Manufacturing Company of Canton, Ohio, should be used. This, as will be noted, holds the flitch at the proper angle. Another dog for plain and quartersawing is the Class' Improved Knights's Patent Duplex Mill dog (see figure 18A) manufactured by the Canton Saw Company, of Canton, Ohio.

FIG. 18A.
CLASS'
IMPROVED
KNIGHT'S PATENT DUPLEX
MILL DOG

The object of the mill is to make good lumber. In building it this fact should be the chief consideration. Sufficient machinery should be installed to take care of this end. It should be simple and accurate to attain the desired object by the most direct route and with the least demand on the power possible. Each addition means not only that much more demand on the power but that much more machinery to get out of order and to be kept in repair. The mill should be kept running steadily while it is running. A mill depreciates about 10 percent per annum under ordinary running. No one has ever been able to figure how fast it depreciates if shut down for any length of time.

FIG. 19. PORTABLE SAWMILL MANUFACTURED BY AMERICAN SAWMILL MACHINERY COMPANY

CHAPTER IV

SAWING FOR GRADE*

I have stated in a former chapter that the question asked at the close of the day is, "How much did you cut?" This question is, of course, all right as the volume of business must be kept up but the question should be qualified and the average grade considered as well as the cut. In these discussions we take the view that in the average mill grade is sacrificed to quantity; that more time and thought are constantly spent on keeping up the cut or increasing it than are spent in studying the logs and putting them through with a view to getting the best grades out of them they are capable of producing. I have been to many mills where there was not a man on the job who knew anything about the grading of the stock they were sawing. I should be glad to know that this article reaches a number of them and be found sufficiently interesting to be studied and create the desire to know more of the details of their own business.

A sawmill operator ought to have at least $4 a thousand net margin on his stock and the only way for him to figure his net margin is to know the value of the average grade of his lumber. The only way to know this value is to know the grades. [NOTE: The figures in the tables that follow were made in the fall of 1914.] Suppose, for example, we had a pine deal like the following:

	Mill run.
Value of stumpage	$ 2.50
Logging, stump to log deck	4.75
Saw bill	2.25
Stacking, carrying and loading	1.50
Cost in car	$11.00

Assuming that $4 a thousand is the minimum margin on which a deal could be operated to be considered profitable an average price of $15 would have to be obtained, which could be obtained as follows:

15 percent B and better @ $24	$ 3.60
40 percent No. 1 common @ $18	7.20
35 percent No. 2 common @ $10	3.50
10 percent No. 3 common @ $7	.70
100 percent	$15.00

If the cut could be increased and this $15 average maintained, then it would be all right to increase the cut but it requires careful figuring to be assured that it is maintained. The inference is that it would not be because when he is hurried all the time the sawyer does not study his log to turn it to best advantage; he rushes boards on the edgerman, who in turn has not time to study his board, and slips it through the edger hit or miss. The trimmerman has the same difficulty. The grader, if any, is rushed too; puts the wrong mark on the board and it winds up in the wrong pile on the yard.

Now suppose the logging crew sends in any kind of logs, and the mill crew does not work for grade, and the final grading of the lumber drops is as follows:

5 percent B and better @ $24	$ 1.20
20 percent No. 1 common @ $18	3.60
50 percent No. 2 common @ $10	5.00
25 percent No. 3 common @ $7	1.75
100 percent	$11.50

Here the average drops down perilously near cost. A day's shutdown in a week would make an actual loss, but unless the grades were known and watched the management would not know it was losing money until the stock was shipped out and it then saw that the stock

[*This article was written in 1914 and based on conditions and prices prevailing at that time.—Editor.]

averaged only cost or less. This illustration could be carried out indefinitely to show different situations that may arise, but the foregoing will suffice to show the importance of knowing what the stock costs put in the car and what the average price obtained is going to be.

If I know that my stock is costing me $11 loaded into cars, and I know the percentage of grades it is running then I can figure exactly what I will have to have per thousand for each grade to net me the average price of $15. If one grade is reduced 50 cents a thousand it reduces the average in proportion. If the B and better had to be reduced 50 cents the average could be maintained by securing 25 cents a thousand more for the No. 2 common. If the average price of $15 could not be maintained on account of fall in market prices then two other courses are open still to maintain the $4 margin. One is reducing the cost, the other is raising the grade. Study the different departments and endeavor to secure a 50-cent reduction. Using our illustration I would begin to work first on the logging and see if I could not cut that $4.75 down to $4.50. I would then study the saw bill and see if I could cut 25 to 50 cents off of that. If the minimum of cost and the maximum of service, a very rare condition, had already been reached the desired end could be effected by running a half hour extra a day without extra pay.

I have stated that $4 is small enough margin on which to figure a sawmill deal. Many concerns might think this is too much; others too little. As a rule where one can figure $4 in the final count he will not actually get more than $2, and the man who operated on a figured margin of only $2 would lose money if he had any serious mishaps, and these must be counted on in all deals. Another point in figuring margins is that in most all cases it is assumed that the deal is going to run 300 days in the year and that there will be no bad luck. Sawmill men do not figure enough on what they will do in a shutdown. The result is they are never ready to shut down when the best judgment of the best men is to shut down. I would urge more thought devoted to this matter and in figuring margins; therefore it must be remembered that what is made in the running time must also take care of the time that must be lost in inevitable shutdowns. The thinner the margin on which the mill is operating when it is going the sooner it will be eaten up by the expense that can not be cut off when the wheels are still.

Figuring Averages as a Basis for Costs

It must be remembered that in figuring averages the average for a day or a week does not count for anything and may be very misleading and harmful rather than beneficial. It is only an accurate average covering a period of months or years that is worth anything as a basis for costs. The average man will claim this calls for too much detail and too complicated a system. But if it is started right it will work in with the regular routine of the business and amply compensate for any little extra work on the part of the management or one or two of the employees. It should also be taken into account that the green measure and grade as the stock comes from the mill will depreciate 10 percent in grade and 5 to 8 percent in measure when it is shipped out.

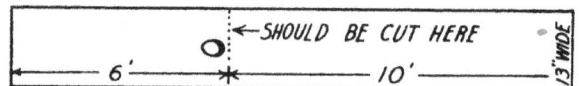

FIG. 20. CUTTING LONG BOARD TO BEST ADVANTAGE

This difference can, of course, be figured accurately if accurate tallies are kept of the green stock that goes on the yard or through the mill and of the dry stock shipped. The chief defects caused in drying are stain, checks, and worms, the last mentioned at certain times during the year and in some climates. Considering these things it can readily be seen that the man who figures on a $2 margin takes a long chance of ever seeing his $2. A fluctuation of more than $2 often occurs in the market, which, in addition to the other chances he is taking, would soon wipe out the margin of the operator who was working on less than $4. This, of course, is a matter of judgment and depends upon the size of the deal, the value of the timber and manufactured product, and the money and ability behind the deal. It would appear that cheap woods like gum, hemlock and pine could be handled more closely than higher priced woods, such as poplar, white pine and oak. As a rule, however, the cheaper woods are subject to greater fluctuations, especially when figured on proportionate values, and thus the margin of profit is the sooner wiped out.

Cost of Cutting Gum Lumber

Owing to the increasing production and use of gum and the lack of correct information and methods of handling I will devote some space in the succeeding chapters particularly to gum. I once heard a prominent southern millman make the statement that all the gum in the country would be sawed up and nobody would make a cent out of it. But that was before the inception of the Gum Lumber Manufacturers' Association and before the attention that it is now receiving was paid to the wood.

Owing to the comparatively low prices of gum it is especially advised that cost figures be kept because this wood during the last few years has been subject to more fluctuations than any other that I know.

Suppose, for example, we have a gum deal like the following:

Value of stumpage	$1.00
Logging, stump to log deck	4.25
Saw bill	2.25
Stacking, carrying and loading	1.75
Cost in car	$9.25

To secure a $4 average on this stock it would have to run something like the following, which looks like a reasonable estimate:

5 percent 1 and 2 red gum, $26	$ 1.30
20 percent No. 1 common red gum, $16	3.20
5 percent sap gum box boards, $20	1.00
20 percent 1 and 2 sap gum, $15	3.00
25 percent No. 1 common sap gum, $11	2.75
25 percent No. 2 and No. 3 common, $8	2.00
100 percent	$13.25

Now $13.25 looks like a low enough average, but it is higher than the average mill is getting for gum. Moreover, except in certain sections, gum will not run 25 percent and better No. 1 common and better red. It will run probably 10 to 15 percent and in some sections none at all, being all sap gum. A sap gum deal would run about as follows:

5 percent box boards, 13-17, $20	$ 1.00
20 percent 1 and 2 sap gum, $15	3.00
40 percent No. 1 common sap, $11	4.40
35 percent No. 2 and No. 3 common, $8	2.80
100 percent	$11.20

In this second illustration it can readily be seen that there would be a margin of barely $2 and a slump in the market that would reduce the average selling price or a spell of bad weather that would increase the manu-

facturing price would soon bring the two figures together if they did not show an actual loss. I am putting the cost of the stock loaded into the car at $9.25. I have seen it loaded into cars, mill run, at a cost of $8, but that is exceptional. I believe a fair average would be $10. When the cost of gum in the car gets over an average of $10 the manufacturer should know something about selling it or he will find himself getting around a

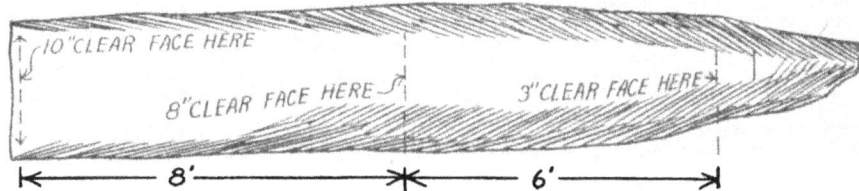

FIG. 21. ANOTHER METHOD OF CUTTING BOARD TO BEST ADVANTAGE

$10 average for his lumber. During the last year considerable gum was sold that did not average the manufacturer $10 a thousand.

The best average price can be secured where the logs run more to red, as it will be seen that the red commands the best price, and if logs can be secured that will produce 25 percent or more No. 1 common and better red then the average goes up. The Mississippi Delta gum produces the largest percentage of red. The gum of Alabama, Georgia and the Atlantic coast runs more to sap, though the red produced while it is less in proportion is just the same in quality and color, and no one has ever said that the delta gum was any better except perhaps someone from the delta. In considering gum stumpage as an investment, whether it is red gum or sap gum is the main thing to consider. About the only way to tell the percentage of red it will run is to saw some of it. As a rule it takes a log 24 inches or over to produce a profitable percentage of red. If none of it can be cut then size is the best way to judge it. The large trees with the dark, deeply grooved bark will run to red gum, while the medium and smaller trees with smoother, lighter bark will run to sap.

I present the illustrations of costs and percentages of grades not so much for the purpose of giving information as to what the stock should cost in the car or the average price it should bring as to show how to arrive at what it does cost and does bring. If a man knows what it is costing and if he has the percentage of grades it is running he will know what he will have to have to make money, if he has decided what it takes to make it. His gum might cost him $11 in the car, in which case he should have an average of $14 to $16. Some firms get their average up to between $17 and $20, but they do it by having sufficient stock to carry all grades and thicknesses on hand and by maintaining a selling force that gets the last dollar from the consuming trade.

To raise the grade one must begin at the stump and see that No. 1 logs are sent to the mill, prepared in a No. 1 manner. Then spend some time with sawyer, edgerman and trimmerman to see that they turn, edge and trim the stock to the very best advantage for grade. Suppose the desired average or margin still could not be secured? Then the deal had better be shut down until conditions improve.

It will be seen that to know what one is doing it is necessary to know, first, what the manufactured stock is costing, mill run, loaded into cars, and, second, the percentage of each grade.

I would recommend that the sawyer, edgerman and trimmerman all be required to know the grades of the different woods they saw. They need not be competent to make final shipments, but should know the grades at least in a general way. They should know that ones and twos are 6 inches and wider, 8 feet and longer, and the maximum defects that are admitted; that No. 1

common is 4 inches and wider by 6 feet and longer, and should cut two-thirds clear or better; that No. 2 common is 3 inches and wider and cuts 50 per cent or better clear or sound, as the case may be. Copies of the grading rules can readily be secured from the secretaries of the associations and a copy of the grading rules of the kinds of lumber being manufactured should certainly be in the hands of and be memorized by each of the above mentioned employees as well as by the regular inspectors.

A sawyer will come along and be touted and recommended as the best in the country when his chief qualifications will be his ability to jerk the carriage back and forth in a hurry without striking the bumper or to turn the log with the nigger without stopping the carriage—mere mechanical operations perfected by long practice. I would rather teach my lumber inspector to handle these levers and then I would have a sawyer. It is generally acknowledged that the sawyer is the most important man in the mill, but I think the edgerman is just about as important for he can make or lose a dollar a thousand on the average according as he is proficient or deficient. A competent edgerman will offset many of the blunders made by an incompetent sawyer, and on the other hand a poor edgerman will undo much of the good work of a competent sawyer. To obtain the best grade out of a log there should be thorough accord and understanding between these two men. They should not only know the grades but should discuss with each other and the trimmerman how to manipulate the log and the boards to get the best out of them, knowing that they can make or lose their day's wages on one log by carelessness. Times innumerable instead of having the edgerman rip out all of the defects it pays to let the board go to the trimmer and have a wider, shorter board than a narrow, long one. For example, in figure 20 this board is 16 feet long by 13 inches wide. It contains all the sap admitted in the best grade and will not carry in addition the knot shown in the center. This knot is too near the middle to be ripped out and leave a clear 6-inch piece; moreover, the 6-inch piece, if otherwise clear, would have too much sap in it, so instead of having the edgerman handle this board let it go to the trimmerman and he can make one 6-foot No. 1 common and one 10-foot good board. If the knot were further down toward the middle he could make two 8-foot boards, one good and one No. 1 common or No. 2, as the case may be. It pays to cut 16-foot boards in two, either 8- or 10-foot lengths if one end of the board is one grade higher than the other, but the edgerman and trimmerman must know the grades in order to determine this. Also the logs must be running sufficiently long to admit of this reduction to shorter lengths without running below the percentage of 14 and 16 required.

In the edging and trimming of slab boards is where a knowledge of the grades is essential and where considerable judgment can be exercised, and where as a rule considerable waste is caused. Where the clear face tapers off into bark toward the little end it frequently pays to count on only half the length and make a wider, short board rather than a narrow, long one. Sometimes, as in figure 21, it will pay to run the board to the trimmerman, let him cut it in two and then return the small end for edging again.

In this slab the edgerman should set the machine at about 8 inches so as to get an 8-inch board out of the wide end. The trimmerman will cut off a clear board 8 feet long. The small end can be returned to the edgerman and he can then get a 3- or 4-inch clear strip, 6 feet or longer, that will grade No. 1 or No. 2 common, as the case may be. Suppose that in this way one board 8" x 8' and one board 4" x 6' were secured; they would total 7 board feet whereas if the edgerman set the machine 6 inches for one longer board and if the trimmerman cut off at 10 feet the board would contain 5 board feet, whereas if he could squeeze it up to 12 feet long it would contain but 6 board feet, a gain

of one or two board feet in this slab of the same grade of lumber. This is but one illustration of various problems that arise. A different situation is faced on every board. If the men know the grades at a glance they can tell without the least hesitancy the best way in which to handle a board. It might appear in reading over this that it sounds all right on paper but the ordinary sawmill crew can not be taught to put it into practice. This is not the fact and it is where many operators fall down. The management figures more on the little time that might be lost in training the men than it does on the lasting and continual gain that would result from their training. Let the boards come gradually from the saw, and not two or three on top of each other and another pile before the first is disposed of. The edgerman can thus have a few seconds in which to judge his board and adjust his saws. He can make a sign to the trimmerman, if necessary, as to how he intends the board to be trimmed. In occasional stops let these men study boards to see if they have put them through the machines to best advantage. When the mill is shut down and there is shipping being done let these men—the sawyer, edgerman and trimmerman—go on the yard and watch the lumber being graded from the pile. Let them do some of the work. Bear in mind that they can not know too much about a board.

These men should also know comparative values of grades. For example, in oak where the difference in the price between No. 1 common and ones and twos is from $15 to $20 it pays to trim four feet off the end of a No. 1 common board if it can thus be raised to good. In pine or gum where the difference is from $4 to $8 it pays to cut off two feet only.

Time was when stumpage was cheaper and more accessible that the sawmill man could afford to run his business without thought of waste; but that is in the past and the man who today runs a sawmill to profit is the one who studies the closest utilization of his raw material; who knows what it is costing him to do business and knows before it is sold what he will get for his product. I will admit that much that is written is theory and is hard to put into actual practice, but the fault I find with so many sawmill operators is that they simply pronounce it all theory and run on, getting only 50 percent efficiency out of their organization.

All the recommendations I have made are put into actual practice by the mills that are being properly managed. The number of them is increasing. I recently visited one mill sawing hardwood where the edgerman had studied the hardwood rule. I do not mean here the rules in the book, but the actual measuring stick. He learned that in edging 16-foot lumber instead of making a board say, even 13 inches wide which would measure 17 board feet, by edging it a little fuller or up close to 13½ inches wide it contains 18 board feet. This is not a theory. It is what I saw a man practicing. This same man has also on his yard a little gasoline engine with a rip and cut-off saw, making it convenient for the shipping crew to rework boards marked by the inspector for improvement in the grade. Many times boards are not thus reworked because it is not convenient. This is not a large mill either as it produces and ships about one car of lumber a day.

Which End of the Log First?

There has been considerable discussion in the lumber papers as to the proper end of the log to bring into the mill. I recommend the small end first first, last, and all the time. In case of a chain haul-up out of a pond the small end will certainly catch and pull up the best. The sawyer can judge a whole lot better what he can get out of a log from the small end than he can the butt. In case of split or hollow butts the deck man can signal the sawyer, calling his attention to the imperfection. The slab tripper can handle better slabs coming to him small end first, and certainly the edgerman can gage his slab boards better small end ahead. The arguments put up in favor of butt end first are that the log might be gritty and that the saw does not have to scrape down a gritty face, thus taking the edge off the teeth before going into the wood; that where band saws are used the offset may not work immediately and a sliver on the log will jerk off the saw on a quick return; that the timber opens better butt end first. I think the advantages of the small end first offset these apparent disadvantages. In running a river mill with which I was once connected the men preferred to bring

20 inches or better, I recommend the following method as shown in figures 22, 23 and 24.

I stated that this method is best adapted to logs of 20 inches and over. For small logs it makes the lumber too narrow. It necessitates the edgerman edging at least one edge of every board, but it has the advantage of throwing the sap all on one edge except in the first cut, and the boards shown in figures 23 and 24 will not be subject to cupping as much as those made from figure 22, on account of reaching only half way across the log. The boards marked with a cross will be

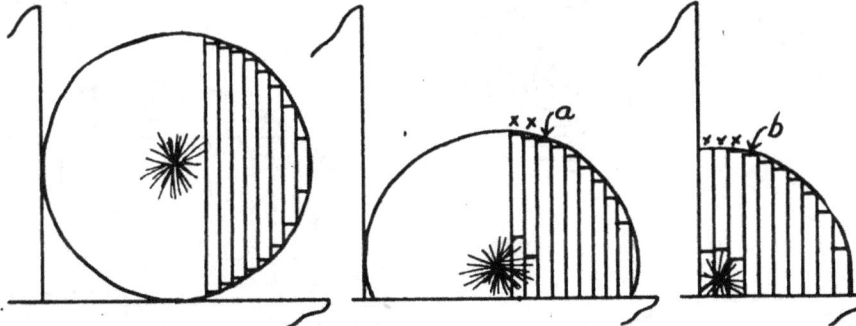

FIG. 22—FIRST CUT   FIG. 23—SECOND CUT   FIG 24—THIRD CUT

up the butt end first, especially if the log was hollow, because catfish went up into the hollows to rest or hide or for some purpose, and during a season the men caught several weighing 75 to 100 pounds each. If the small end had come first the fish would have dropped out. Hence a hundred pounds of fish paid to bring up the butt end first.

For the average deal, unless there are some special or exceptional conditions, I think the best results can be obtained in the long run by bringing the small end into the mill first.

To get the grade out of the log the sawyer must first turn it right. Here again haste stands in the way of quality. It takes a half minute or so to judge a log, and as it opens up it should be considered care-

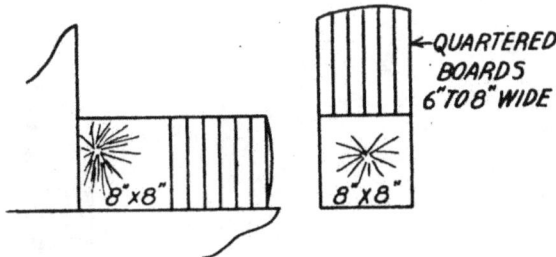

FIG. 25 AND FIG. 26

fully by the sawyer to be turned to best advantage. Unless the sawyer knows the grade, however, he might just as well hurry it through so as to try to make up in quantity what he lacks in quality.

I will show some general methods of turning logs but it must be remembered that in this as well as in so many other conditions of lumbering a fixed rule can not be laid down, and that is why it is essential that the men know the grades and they will then know when to depart from the general rule and when to adhere to it.

A good rule for the sawyer to follow is to turn the log every time he sees a better face than the one on which he is sawing.

In plain sawing oak logs of good average size, say

quartered. The figures shown assume the heart to be edged off and thrown away. For boxing the heart handle as in figure 22. In the second cut stop with the board marked A and turn down for the third cut the same as in figure 24, but stop with board marked B, which should leave the remaining cant 6, 7 or 8 inches, according to the square desired. This cant should then be handled as in figure 25 for plain sawing or the square could be cut off and the remainder quartered as in figure 26.

Quarter-sawing means to saw parallel with the medullary rays, which are rays radiating from the heart of the log outward. The term quarter-sawing comes from the fact that to saw parallel with these rays through the greater part of the log it is necessary practically to quarter the log by splitting it in half and then again splitting these halves. Any line sawn directly toward the center will produce the quartered effect, but it will be noted that to saw lines towards the center it is necessary to split the log up into quarters and to turn these quarters on their backs. By this method of sawing, certain woods, especially oak and sycamore, show a very beautiful figure. The more nearly the lines can be sawn directly toward the heart the more perfect will be the quarter-sawing. Thus in figure 26 the middle board or the one reaching directly into the center of the log is a perfectly quartered board. Oak is more generally quartered than any other wood because of the figure it shows, but many other woods are quartered or rift sawn (a synonymous term) because a quartered board will stay straighter and hold its shape under tests that a plain sawn board will not stand. In ordinary hardwoods for plain sawing a sixteenth full is necessary for the lumber to dry out a plump inch; in thicker stock an eighth. In quarter-sawing the boards should be sawn 1⅛ full for inch stock, ₁₆-inch on 5 and 6/4, and ¼-inch on 2-inch stock. Quartered lumber shrinks in thickness more than plain. Plain shrinks more in width than quartered.

Methods of quarter-sawing oak and sawing edge grain or rift flooring have been discussed in the AMERICAN LUMBERMAN and I will now show these methods with illustrations as they have previously appeared, which are deserving of the closest study. The article mentioned is as follows:

In figure 27 the small diagram illustrates the ordinary method of squaring a log and the saw cuts on the upper half of the larger figure show the relation of the circular annual rings to the boards produced by this method. The board "G" is truly quarter-sawed. Those next to it, up to "B," are practically quarter-sawed at the outer edges, but have a section which is truly flat-sawed in the center of the board, and this proportion of the flat to quartered or partly quartered stock increases in the boards toward the outward edge "b." The lines "ab" and "cd" show how the log is usually

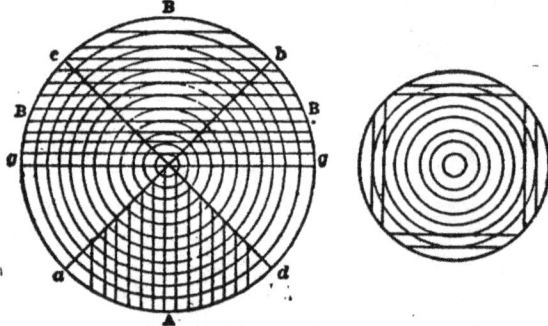

FIG. 27—QUARTER-LOG METHOD OF QUARTER-SAWING

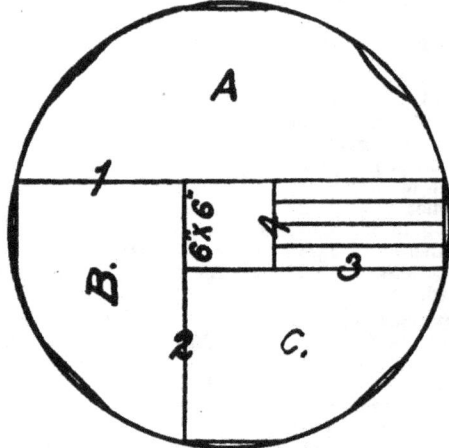

FIG. 28—OPENING THE LOG, THE HEART BOXED

split into quarters for quarter-sawing, each quarter then being turned on its back and sawed, as in "a." This produces truly quarter-sawed stock at the center of the wedge and makes a sufficiently close approximation for most purposes, except at the extreme corners.

A method of quarter-sawing which produces a larger pro-

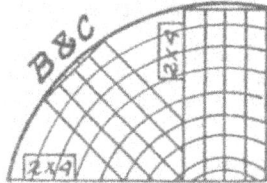

FIG. 29—SAWING B AND C, FIG. 28

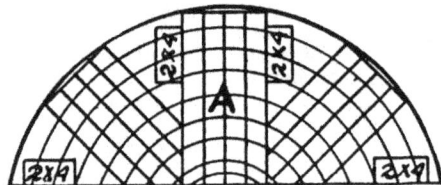

FIG. 30—SAWING SECTION A FROM FIG. 28

portion of more exactly quarter-sawed stock is represented by figures 28, 29 and 30. Figure 28 shows how the heart is boxed and "B" and "C" from this diagram are then manipulated, as in figure 29, while the portion "A" of the log is handled as in figure 30.

Figures 31 and 32 relate to the sawing of edge-grain flooring from yellow or norway pine, and are not of interest to this inquirer, but are reproduced because of their interest to others. In figure 31 the log is first approximately squared, and cuts 1 to 5 are then taken through the center. The cants "a" and "b" are then piled one on top of the other and sawed together, as indicated. Approximately all of the lumber within the inner circle is sufficiently quarter-sawed to answer the purposes of edge-grain flooring. Figure 32 shows a different way of handling the log after being squared, the heart being boxed and used for dimension, while the two pieces 4 by 12 and the two pieces 4 by 4 are sawn into flooring strips.

Figures 33 and 34 show the same method of quarter-sawing as is indicated in figure 27, the quartered log being turned

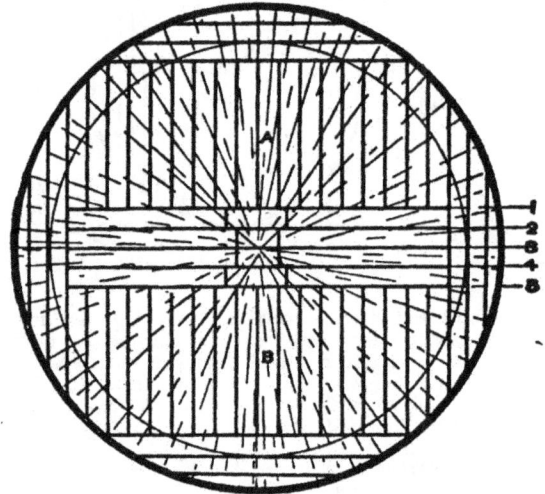

FIG. 31—SAWING YELLOW PINE EDGE GRAIN FLOORING

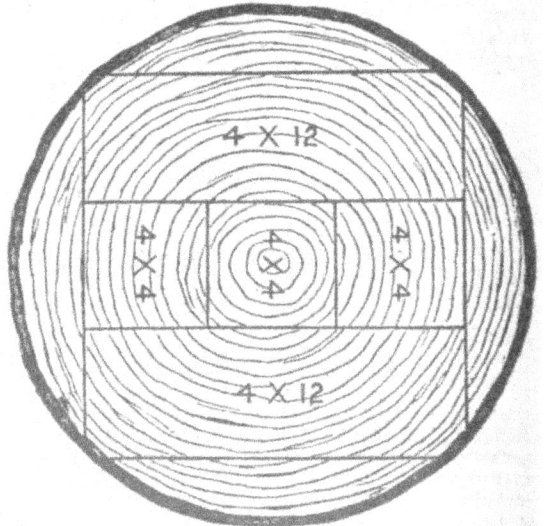

FIG 32—ANOTHER EDGE GRAIN FLOORING METHOD BOXING HEART

on its back and sawed through without changing position. These figures are intended to illustrate the effect upon the figure of the resulting boards if the log, as in figure 34, has only half as many medullary rays. It might be remarked, parenthetically, that an oak tree of a given botanical description does not vary much in this regard, whatever may have been its growth environment. The proportion in volume of the medullary rays is pretty constant to the other or vertical cells, although it is possible that a larger proportion may be of the small and inconspicuous variety and a smaller proportion of the broad thick rays which are most prominent in quartered figure. Where a number of different kinds botanically are commercially lumped together as "white oak"[2] or "red oak," there may be considerable variation in the number of medullary rays.

Figures 33 and 34 were published and commented upon May 30, 1908, as emphasizing the need of careful selection of

narrower wedge all the boards approximate more closely to true quarter-sawing. Yet it should be remembered that at some point in the process the increase in labor and waste overbalances the gain in quality.

On October 30, 1909, figures 35 and 36 were published to illustrate the sawing methods used by the Clarke & Baker Company, Ilion, N. Y., figure 36 of course representing plain-sawing. A little study of figure 35 will show that the log, in effect, is divided into 12 wedge-shaped sections, each of

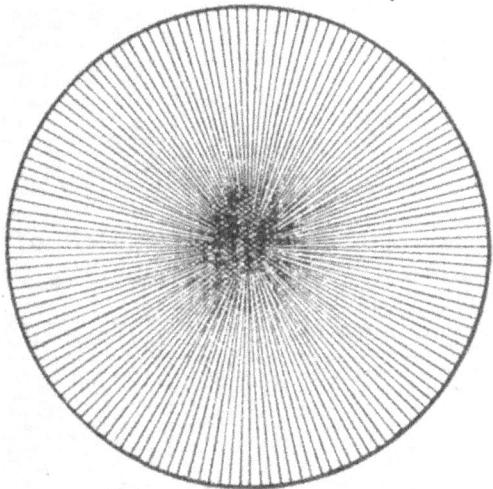

THIS CANT CAN BE GANG-SAWED

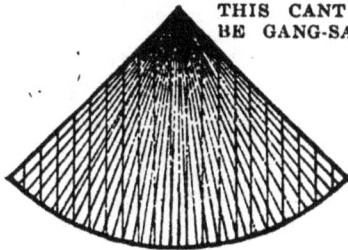

FIG. 33—EFFECT OF CLOSE RAYS, QUARTER-LOG METHOD

FIG. 34—EFFECT OF SCANTIER RAYS, REDUCING FIGURE

wood for quarter-sawing purposes. The Mengel Box Company, in the issue of July 4, 1908, commented upon these figures and in substance stated that if the poorer log shown by figure 34 had been sawn into wedges of one-eighth instead of one-quarter and each of these wedges had been sawn into lumber, the average resulting figure of the boards would have been superior to those shown from the better log in figure 33 by the quartering method. This, of course, is because in the

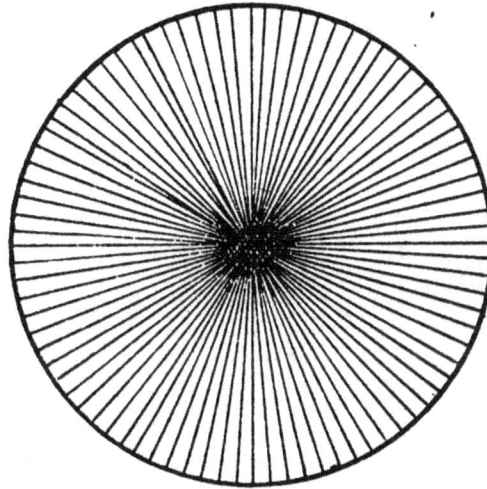

which is sawn up parallel to one of its wedge faces. As regards the product this is equivalent to sawing the log into six wedges and sawing each wedge parallel with its center line. Inasmuch as the Mengel method divides the log into eight wedges instead of six, sawing each parallel with the center, it approximates true quartering more closely than does diagram 35.

In the above remarks it is not assumed that the log is actually divided into 12 wedges as an initial operation, because undoubtedly each half of the log is progressively canted or tilted upon the block in the method of sawing figured by this diagram.

There are various other methods of quartering lumber

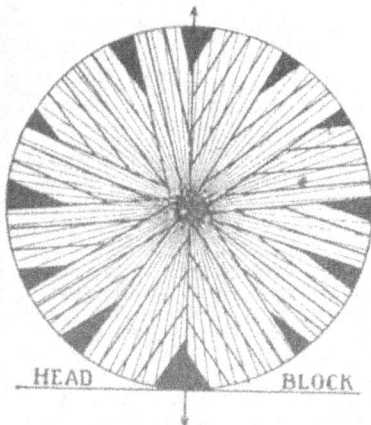

HEAD BLOCK

FIG. 35—QUARTER-SAWING BY SUCCESSIVE TILTS OF HALF-LOG

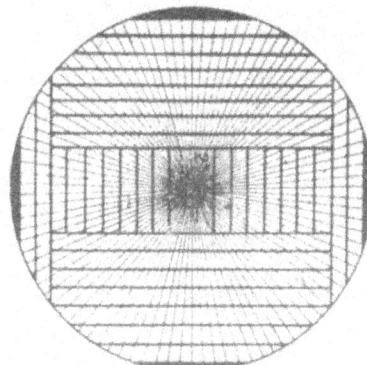

FIG. 36—PLAIN-SAWING DIAGRAM

besides those indicated and the quartering of lumber must in each case be a compromise between the cost of a given method and the quality of the product. The higher the percentage of quartered lumber secured, the greater is the amount of waste in trimming off oblique edges and the greater must be the expense of sawing, in the numerous manipulations of the log.

The reason quarter-sawed lumber is worth more than plain is not alone because it may be figured and will stay straighter, but it takes more time and causes considerably more waste than plain sawing. Rift flooring is worth more than flat grain because it requires much more care and causes more waste in manufacturing; it will lay perfectly flat and, the edge of the grain being

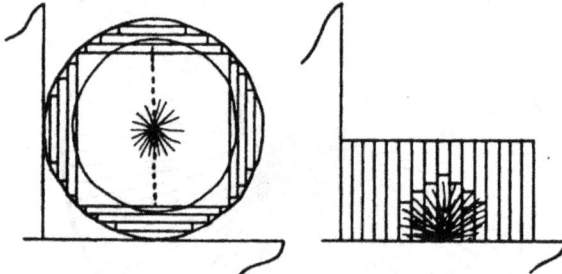

FIGS. 37 AND 38—METHOD OF QUARTERING RED GUM

exposed instead of the flat surface, it will wear much longer and will not sliver or become rough from wear or scrubbing.

As the object in quarter-sawing gum is to obtain quartered red the sap should first be removed or practically removed and then the red part can be split open and the heart face turned down, sawing it right through. The other half is handled the same way. As the object of quartering red gum is to obtain a rift effect rather than figure it does not have to be worked

and the two should as nearly as possible be separated, observing from the rules how much sap a red board will admit. For this reason, as shown, it is best first to go around the log removing the sap and then saw the red as another log. It is recommended that the slab-tripper or off-bearer send the board to the edgerman with the widest red face up, as the rules require only one red face in red gum.

Wagon box boards are, in most woods, worth more than ones and twos, but in gum wagon box boards are made chiefly from the sap and are not worth as much as one and two red, there being a difference of about $8 a thousand in favor of the one and two red. Care should therefore be taken that too much good red does not go into the wide box boards and in an effort to get sap gum box the percentage of good red might be reduced. The log should first be considered. If it runs chiefly to sap, saw for sap gum box boards. If it has a thin sap and runs to red work for No. 1 common and better red.

The method of sawing for wagon box boards is as illustrated in figures 39, 40 and 41.

During the last few years in the South the pine mills have been sawing their hardwoods as they clean up the land and managers have not taken much pains to instruct their crews nor to learn themselves how to turn or to handle a hardwood log. In ordinary plain sawing a pine log it is all right to square the log to 8, 10 or 12 inches and then gang-saw it, but in hardwood this will not work because the heart of all hardwood logs is defective and if the defect runs from one end of the board to the other it reduces the grade to No. 2 and No. 3 common no matter how good it might otherwise be. If the sawyer ran straight through the log it would appear that the heart centers could be ripped out by the edgerman but he probably does not know as much about it as the sawyer and, moreover, if the board had the bark on each edge he would require four saws

FIGS. 39, 40 AND 41—METHOD OF SAWING FOR WAGON BOX BOARDS

as much toward the center as oak or sycamore, where the object is to obtain figure, although quartered red gum will show a ribbony figure, much resembling mahogany, and an experienced man can easily distinguish a plain from a quartered board. The method of quartering red gum is illustrated in figures 37 and 38.

The red part could be sawed up as a whole without splitting and then the edgerman could split the boards and rip out the heart, but better results can be had by splitting. As this method does not quarter the outside boards on either cant they should be separated and piled with the plain. The red part of the log, where it is large enough, could be sawed the same as in the illustration given for sawing large oak, and any logs where width is not an essential can be turned to advantage by that method. (See figures 20, 21 and 22.)

It should be remembered that there are practically two different woods in a gum tree, red gum and sap gum,

in the board to edge it and take out the center and he would not put the four saws in it right, even if he had them in his edger.

Assuming that the pine crew will not learn the hardwood grades, about the best way for the crew to saw hardwood is to have the sawyer turn the log according to the illustrations given for turning the larger oak, as in figures 20, 21 and 22, and those given for sawing box boards, according to the size and character of the log, remembering that hardwood runs to random and not to stock widths; that they should get as much clear lumber 6 inches and wider as possible and that heart centers should as far as possible be turned to one edge of the boards and edged off by the edgerman or, if they come in the center, ripped out in a three- or four-inch piece and the piece sent to the fire doors instead of the yard.

Frequently where there are only one or two knots on a log the log should be turned so these knots will come in the edges of two or three boards, rather than in the middle of five or six. Thus in figure 42 I would turn the knots back to the blocks in placing the log on the carriage; saw into the heart, then turn it flat down and saw it up as in figure 43.

length of the log. Then turn this back to the blocks and saw until a straight line is reached again. In this manner the edgerman and trimmerman can make some short boards from the middle on one side and from the ends on the other, whereas if the log were sawn straight

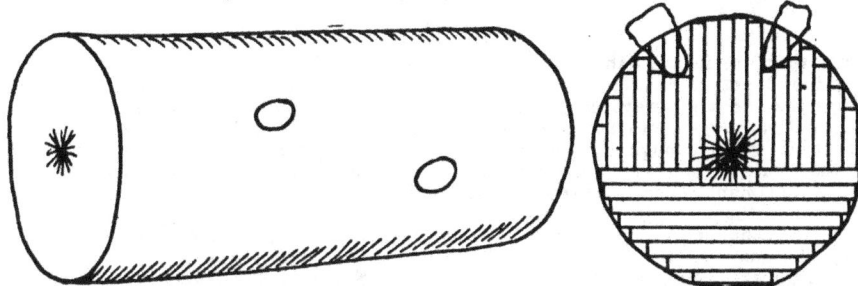

FIG. 42, SHOWING KNOTS, AND FIG. 43, SHOWING METHOD OF ELIMINATION

Referring to figure 41, sawing for box boards, suppose there was a knot on the back side of the log noted by the cross mark and it looked like a deep knot the best way to turn the cant after sawing into the heart would be as illustrated in figure 44.

FIG. 44—TURNING LAST CANT ON FIG. 41, IN CASE OF KNOT ON BACK SIDE

Of course if the log is full of knots there is no way to suggest as the best method of procedure, except for the sawyer to study the log, and if there is no way to get clear lumber try next for sound.

I went into the mill one day when the sawyer had on the carriage a crooked log like that shown in figure 45. He asked me what I would do with it.

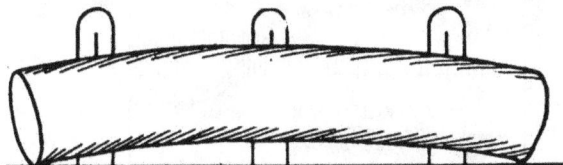

FIG. 45—CROOKED LOG ON CARRIAGE

As the log happened to be 16 feet long I told him to rip it straight through just in the position he had it on the carriage. I had the boards run first to the trimmerman and cut in two, making two 8-foot boards, and then had them edged. If, however, the log had not been 16 feet long it would not have paid to handle it in this manner. For a shorter crooked log I would suggest turning the bow out, instead of placing it on the carriage as shown in the figure, thus making some short boards until a straight line is reached the full

up as in figure 45 the short stock would be wasted by the edger. This is just a suggestion as to what to do with a crooked log when it gets in the mill, but a properly instructed logging crew will not permit it to come into the mill.

Practically every log, just as has almost every board, has one face better than the other. Sawyers can readily tell which is the best side of their log and place it on the carriage so as to work this good side to best advantage. In sawing tapering logs, where the taper is more than 6 inches—that is, where the butt is 6 inches or more in diameter than the small end—it is best to set out the small end so as to make the first cut parallel with the face of the log instead of beginning at the butt end and taking off short pieces. This will make straight grained instead of biased grained boards. Saw in until the heart is reached on the small end. It is well to saw about two 1-inch boards beyond the heart on the small end and let the trimmerman cut off this short end of heart shake. Then turn the flat side back to the blocks, running the small end out again so the bark face will be parallel with the saw. The sawyer can use his judgment whether to saw this piece right on up or turn it once or twice more, according to his log, leaving either a four-sided or two-sided wedge-shaped piece from the butt end of the log. This can be run to the dimension mill for further service or to the wood pile according to the method of the operation. A few feet more lumber and straight grained boards can sometimes be obtained from swell butted or tapering logs by the above described method.

Some observations on sawing are the following:

Do not sacrifice grade to quantity.

Insist that the sawyer, edgerman and trimmerman know the grades.

Fifteen thousand feet at $20 a thousand is better than 20,000 feet at $15 a thousand, even though the money value of the total is the same.

If you want the mill crew to do better offer them a premium for No. 1 common and better. They will get plenty of No. 2 and No. 3 common without a premium.

The sawyer, edgerman and trimmerman can make or lose their wages for the day on a half dozen logs. If it is large enough they can lose it on one.

The edgerman is just as important a man as the sawyer, but he has not been receiving the attention he deserves.

To make money in a sawmill the saw must be kept in the log, but that does not necessarily mean that it should be jammed through and everybody be buried with lumber all the time.

The maxim that "Haste makes waste" was started in a sawmill.

CHAPTER V

YARD AND PILING

Yard

Men do what they are in the habit of doing. If the men are taught and get in the habit of doing things right the things they do are always done right, whereas if they are permitted to get into the careless habit of thinking "that is good enough" anything is good enough and the work is slighted. It depends in the last analysis on the management. If the management passes carelessness without reprimand it can not expect efficiency. But the management does what it is in the habit of doing the same as the laborer. An incompetent manager continues incompetent and a careless crew continue careless until some force outside themselves either sets them to thinking or by some authority they respect works them out of the rut. The manager who does not know can not tell whether the men know or not, and frequently men insist to the manager that they know what they are doing when they know they are doing right when they are not. Many managers do not give the yard and piling the attention they deserve. They think if they can get the lumber through the mill anybody can put it on sticks. The result is that considerable good lumber is ruined by poor sticking on poor pile bottoms. It should be the policy of the management to see that the stock is so handled that when a good board comes away from the trimmer it will remain a good board until it is put into the car.

In laying off the yard the first thing that should be considered is how much lumber will have to be stacked. If we are running a hardwood mill cutting 15,000 feet a day we will have to carry at least four months' run or 100 days' cut on sticks, making 1,500,000 feet. Then if the shipping did not keep pace with the production the stocks would continue to increase and more yard room would be needed. I would suggest lining off the yard so as to have room to carry at least six months' cut on sticks. By planning for this in the beginning the chance is avoided of having to make some sort of a shift for more piling room when it is not convenient and when it may not conform to the general plan of the yard already established, thus requiring more handling and expense.

Next thing to observe is the prevailing winds. Arrange the piles so the prevailing winds will hit them sidewise instead of on the ends. Lumber in the yard will dry more quickly on a windy day than it will on a hot day when there is no wind, but for the wind to do any good it must go through the pile and if it hits the pile on the ends it cannot go through it. The yard should also be high and dry for even then it is hard enough to combat stain. If the yard is in a low, flat place, at certain seasons of the year the lumber will not only stain but the middle of the piles will not dry, remaining soggy and heavy.

Tramways should not be built for a hardwood operation. They are all right for pine, especially where the No. 1 common and better is all put through the kilns and only the excess No. 2 common and dimension stock are run to the yard to be air dried. The argument for the building of trams is that stacks can be run higher and lumber can be stacked down from a tramway much more rapidly than it can be stacked up from the ground. On the other hand, tramways are expensive as a first cost and after a few years expensive to maintain. The lumber will stain from the tramway to the ground, and it is a question whether tramways are a paying investment at all. For certain deals and under certain conditions they are, of course, but this has to be determined by the conditions.

In considering yards and piling, unless otherwise specified, I am writing of the average mill where lumber is air dried and shipped from the yard without being run through the planing mill. A convenient form of yard of this kind is illustrated in figure 46.

If the ground space is available this form of yard can be extended to cover any required space. This arrangement is for a track system, over which trucks carrying 500 feet of green lumber or 1,000 feet of dry may be run by two men. The initial cost of this form of yard is not so great as that for building tramways covering the same space, and the loading will be cheaper. Or the same general plan can be used for hauling on dollies with a horse and without track. I think the track is the most economical in the long run because it will cost more to maintain the road bed for driving than it will to maintain the track. Moreover four men will load as much lumber by this system as four men with a horse and driver by the road system. The following specifications should be observed:

The distance from track to track should be at least 44 feet, which will give 4 feet from track to face of

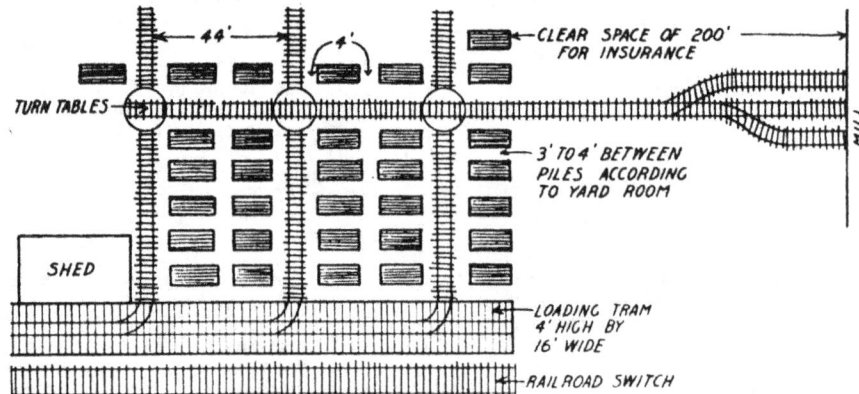

FIG. 46—A CONVENIENT FORM OF YARD

pile, 16 feet for the form and 4 feet between forms at the rear. Piles should be 3, preferably 4, feet apart. This can be determined according to the yard space available. The forms should be built in a straight line all through the yard, giving the air an opportunity to pass through each way.

Forms should be built 12, 14 and 16 feet long, or they may be built all 16 feet with a cross sill at the 12- and 14-foot line for 12- and 14-foot stock. Pile bottoms should be given particular attention as they should not only be solid but the foundations should be so substantial that when the weight is on them they will not settle out of shape. Building forms with concrete foundations are recommended, but they are expensive for the smaller operator. The top of the form should be from 18 inches to 2 feet off the ground in the front. It should have a pitch of at least 1 inch to the lineal foot. A greater pitch is recommended by some authorities but any greater pitch makes rather a steep pile on which to work. A pitch of 1 inch will make a 16-foot form 16 inches lower at the rear than the front. Piles may be 6, 7 or 8 feet wide, the wider the pile the more open the lumber should be stacked. One good method of building bottoms is to take small trees, 8 to 12 inches in diameter, and cut them into blocks, bevelling one end to the desired pitch as illustrated in figure 47.

case may be. By having the machines convenient on the yard for no other purpose but improvement in grade, they will be used for that purpose. The size of the shed should, of course, be in proportion to the stock handled.

Piling

Men have to be trained properly to pile lumber just as they have to be trained to do anything else right. Certain fixed rules should be laid down as to piling because in this department a fixed rule can be observed and there is no need for the men to use judgment as to the proper way to place the board in the pile, there being only one proper way. The best results can be had in stacking by separating the lengths and stacking each length separately but as it requires a good deal of stock and a good deal of space to stack each length of each grade separately, tens and twelves may be stacked together and fourteens and sixteens together. Any eighteens that turn up may be stacked with the sixteens, leaving the back ends stick out, though it is not desirable to have any ends sticking out two feet beyond a stick. A stick should be right on each end of a pile, and at uniform distances, 2 to 4 feet as the case may be, through the pile. Sticks should be directly over each other, extending toward the front ¼ to ½ inch with each succeeding layer. In stacking different lengths in

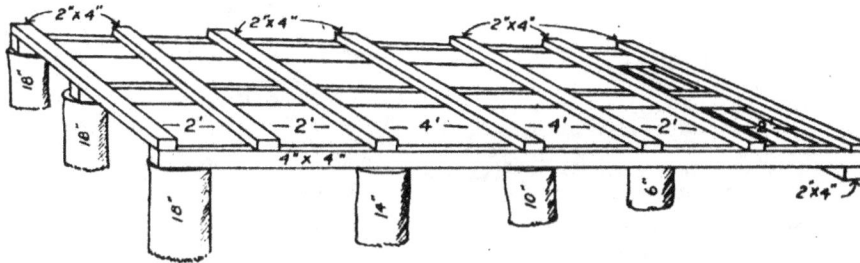

FIG. 47—METHOD OF BUILDING BOTTOMS

For a 16-foot form this would require three blocks 18 inches high, three 14 inches, three 10 inches and three 6 inches. The back end could be a 2x4 laid right on the ground. Then three pieces of 4x4x16 and seven pieces of 2x4 across the top to rest under the stickers would complete the form. This would make the top of the form 24 inches from the ground in the front and 8 inches in the rear, giving the desired pitch of 16 inches for 16 feet.

A shed on the yard is recommended containing stalls in which to place "outs" when shipping instead of uncovering piles and restacking them on the yard. Too many inspectors permit their outs to lie thinking they will pick them up in a day or two when they are loading a car of that kind of stock. They do not get to them and this soon results in a cluttered-up yard. It is best to have a shed and either have several men whose business it is properly to separate and pile the outs in the shed or have the inspector clean up and replace his outs before starting on the next car.

In one of this shed I would recommend a rip- and cut-off saw. Let the inspector mark boards for improvement in grade, putting the marked side up on the trucks. These can be taken off the truck at the car and worked up when the loading crew has time. Where steam or electric power is not convenient, these machines can be run by a gasoline engine. These two machines will constitute the best money savers a man ever put on his operation because, as previously observed, inspectors will not mark boards to improve the grade unless it is convenient to have them worked and the rules will not permit them to be measured inside of marks without being cut or ripped, as the

the same pile sticks may be arranged so they will come at the end of each board as shown in figure 48.

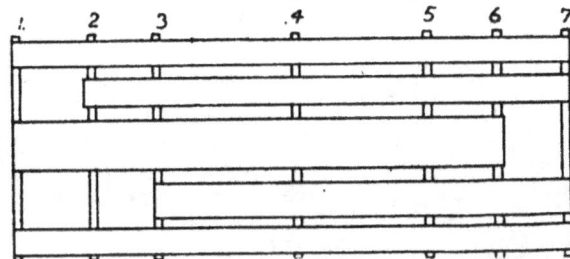

FIG. 48—STACKING DIFFERENT LENGTHS TOGETHER. PILE 6x16 FEET

This shows 12-, 14- and 16-foot boards in the same layer with a stick at the end of each board. The sixteens should be saved for the outside. The eighteens could extend out two feet. The tens could be placed on sticks 2 to 5 or 3 to 6. Two eights could be handled together as one sixteen. This method permits the stacking of eights to eighteens in same pile with sticks at all ends except one end of the eighteens.

It is conceded by the best authorities that the best stick is one inch square. Then it will always have to lie the flat way. I think, however, a 1x2 for the front sticker is advisable as it gives a better opportunity to carry the pile forward. At any rate sticks should be of a uniform thickness. They should be dry when used and should be free from bark. Making sticks from edging strips with the bark on is bad practice and causes damage on the yard. Sawing B and better into strips would be less expensive in the long run than to make them out of bark edgings. Any kind of wood is all right for sticks for stacking any kind provided it is dry wood. No lumber should be stacked on green sticks. Boards should be 4 to 6 inches apart in the layers. It is better to leave more space in a layer than to try to put in another board. Economizing space by stacking lumber closely is not economy. Save space by going up in the air, because the higher the pile goes the better it will dry.

Lumber should be stacked so that the front of the pile runs forward an inch and a half or two inches

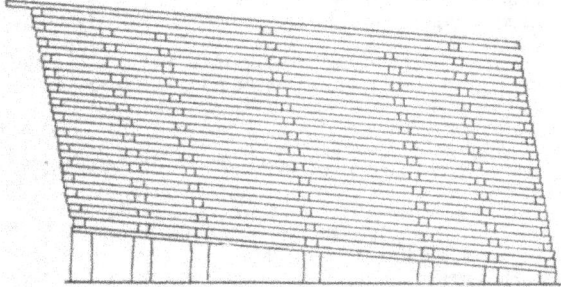

FIG. 49—SHOWING SIDE OF PILE

to the foot, and a properly finished pile will look from the side like figure 49.

Covering on a pile should not be air or water tight as it is the sun that does damage to lumber and not the rain. Covering boards should be two feet longer than the pile, if possible, and should be placed about 3 inches apart, leaving about the same spaces as in the layer below. The object of covering is simply to keep the top layers from curling up and season-checking.

Prevention of Stain

As the method of stacking causes or prevents stain I will take up here the prevention of stain, dealing in particular with gum. If gum logs are sawn from the stump during October to April inclusive, and sent at once to the mill and put on sticks as in figure 51 the sap will not stain and does not have to be put through any process whatsoever. It is impossible, however, to arrange to saw the stock only at that time because those months in which it is best to saw are the worst for logging. But at any time it is recommended that the logs be run promptly through the mill and the lumber put on sticks. Where it is impossible to run the logs through the mill at once, it does not hurt to place them in a pond or to leave the tops on the trees until the leaves wilt. Then when sawn into log lengths the ends of the logs should be creosoted or loraced.

Several manufacturers are successfully combating stain in sap gum by putting the lumber first through a steam box, which can be cheaply fixed up by making a box large enough to hold one kiln truck and then running the exhaust pipe from the engine into the box. The lumber can be left in the steam box from one to several hours, as convenient, and can then be run to the yard or through the kiln as desired. One inch or thinner gum can be successfully kiln dried but I do not recommend kiln drying thicker stock.

The Kraetzer Company, of Chicago, has patented a preparator for the scientific steaming of gum and all other woods as well, claiming that all woods are benefited by the steaming process. This company's method is all right if it can be afforded, for it costs from $7,000 to $9,000 and it is recommended for cuts of 10,000,000 or more a year. The company also discovered that to give the lumber some pitch in the preparator it was necessary to pitch the foundations on the trucks sidewise instead of lengthwise, and with its permission this method illustrated from a page in the company's catalogue is shown, and also the proper method of sticking. This method has the advantage of causing the water to run directly off of each layer after a rain, and it can not be held by the stickers as in other piles. The dirt and sawdust do not accumulate at the angle of the stickers. (See figure 50.)

Most stain is caused by close piling or by lumber not going immediately on sticks. If sap gum or any other wood that is subject to stain is sawn the same day the tree is felled and is put on sticks that same day and stuck in the following manner on an open yard the stain will be a negligible quantity. The loss in grade on account of stain will certainly be less than the cost of any anti-stain process. As sound stain that will surface off is no defect in any grade of sap gum the difference in money value as far as inspection goes is not so great

FIG. 50—METHOD OF GIVING PITCH TO LUMBER, PATENTED BY THE KRAETZER COMPANY OF CHICAGO

between stained and bright lumber, but the appearance of bright lumber is so much more desirable and a number of firms, especially exporters, will not accept badly stained stock.

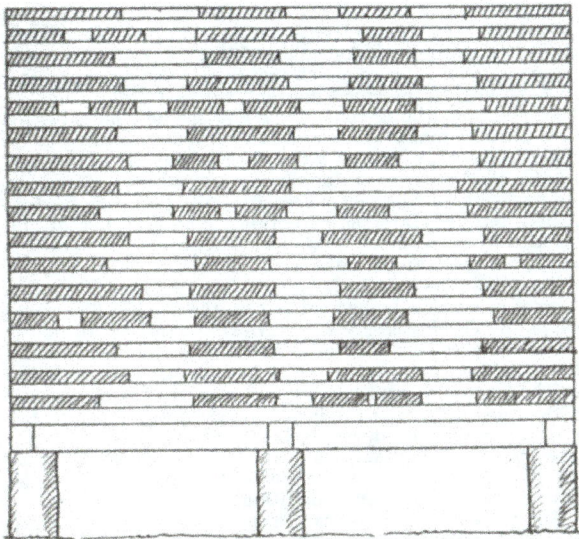

FIG 51—PILING TO PREVENT STAIN

Figure 51 shows the front of the pile. It will be noticed that the boards are arranged in tiers with a flue from top to bottom between each tier. The covering is placed on in the same way, leaving these flues open. Sap gum piled in this way on dry sticks, other conditions being favorable, will dry sufficiently bright to be sold for bright stock and sufficiently straight to suit the most exacting taste. If the box boards 13 to 17 inches are separated they can be stacked in the same way, three tiers in a layer, thirteens on one edge, fourteens and fifteens in the middle and sixteens and seventeens on the other edge. The enemy of stain is air, especially air in circulation, and the way to overcome stain is to give the lumber plenty of air space by separating the piles and then by separating the lumber in the piles. A good rule for air drying lumber is to keep it on sticks a month for each quarter of an inch in thickness.

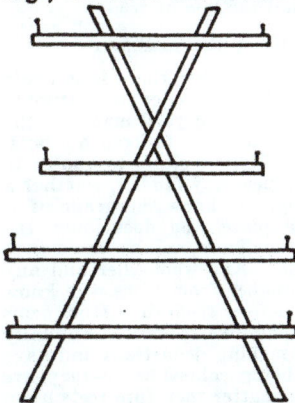

Handling stickers is a serious problem on many yards. They are thrown about in various ways and then have to be gathered up again. A rack between the piles is recommended similar to that shown in figure 52. This is just one end section from which the principle can be seen. For 6-foot stickers the rack should be not over five feet long. These racks can be placed in every other space between piles and much time will be saved in stacking if not in taking down piles.

FIG. 52—STICKER RACK

An Automatic Lumber Stacker

For stacking lumber in high piles a stacking machine has been invented by the Hilke Stacker Company, of Middletown, N. Y. The machine can be used, of course, for taking down as well as for stacking. The method of operation is shown in the accompanying illustration. (See figure 53.)

Some general observations on stacking are as follows:

Lumber should be put on sticks, whether on the kiln trucks or on the yard, immediately after sawing. When the yard crew gets behind with the stacking it is better to shut the mill down until the crew catches up.

Lumber to dry properly, needs space and air. If short of yard space do not crowd the piles together or crowd the layers. Where you have been stacking seventy courses run them up to ninety. The piles can not go too high up in the air. To dry straight, lumber must be stacked straight; to prevent stain it must be stacked in the open.

It is best not to saw thick stock, especially oak and gum, in the summer time, as it will season check no matter how it is stacked.

See that a stick is on the end of every board and keep the sticks over each other, running forward parallel with the front of the pile.

Lumber is not stacked right until the same grade that comes from the mill goes into the car, excepting the natural degrading caused in drying. The percentage of degrading beyond this, which is 8 to 10 percent,

FIG. 53—POWER STACKING MACHINE

determines the percentage of deficiency in stacking and handling through the yard.

If the men are taught to put the piles up right they will vie with each other in seeing which one can put up the most perfect pile.

A prize of a dollar or two a month to the man who put up the most perfect pile during the month would be a good investment.

CHAPTER VI

SELLING THE OUTPUT

The operation is not complete until the lumber is sold and shipped and the account collected. More has been written about salesmanship than any other department of the business. Salesmanship is a science by itself and it is not my purpose to enter into any lengthy discussion of it but I have come into contact with so many of the smaller operators throughout the country, especially in the South, that did not know the first principles about selling their lumber that I am sure some plain talk would be beneficial to them if it were possible to get them to read it. If they would only read it I feel sure at least a percentage would be sufficiently impressed to act upon some of the suggestions, in part at least.

Properly to sell lumber some idea should be had as to its uses. A man who never goes anywhere, who feels that he is so busy and the demands upon him are so great that he must stay right on the job and attend to the manufacture and details of his business, ought not to try to sell his output. The man who sells the stock should know the people to whom he is selling and the class of work they are doing. Where a mill is selling to the wholesale trade only it should know something of the character of the trade the wholesaler works and if wholesalers in placing orders with mills would tell the latter just what the stock is being used for it would many times help in the intelligent filling of an order, where the mill working in the dark gets into trouble.

It should first be determined whether the output is to be sold to the consuming trade or to the wholesale trade. As a rule the small millman or the pine or cypress mill sawing only a limited quantity of hardwood, and that a miscellaneous collection, can not get to the consumer with it. The consumer wants straight carloads of lumber of a certain grade, wants it thoroughly dry, well manufactured stock, and wants it when he wants it and the grade he wants. The manufacturer who does not grade his lumber can not give it to him, hence he must sell his stock either to a wholesaler or to a yard. It is only the mill that separates its grades and is able to ship straight carload lots of one grade of lumber or mixed thicknesses of the same grade, in other words, specified quantities of grade and thickness and then carry the accounts, that is able to work the consuming trade, successfully. If this cannot be done then the consumer can not be reached. If it can be done it is well to learn the needs of a few good factories, say a furniture factory or two, a box factory or two, a few good planing mills, and one or two good wholesale yards, to take care of miscellaneous stock and then manufacture the stock that these customers desire so they can count on getting a certain quantity from your mill and you can count on them taking it. Give the grade in dry, well manufactured lumber, of good average widths, and lengths, and no one can take your trade away. A properly filled order is a far better solicitor for future business than all the scientific salesmanship ever written about in the magazines or taught in the schools. Good lumber sells itself after the sample is delivered. It is the sorry lumber and the low grade that always keep one in hot water. If some of the millmen could be induced to travel more, go thru the factories and be shown the uses to which the lumber is put, and the finished products that are made from it, they could better realize why the consumer has to be particular about the class of stock he receives and why his kick is often justified when the shipper accuses him of being a robber.

Go into a church and look at the pews or into a bank or barber shop and study the finish, and then answer frankly if the interior finish man could put up that kind of work out of the stock you had shipped him. Look at your piano or dining room table and see how much waste each of these manufacturers had before they secured clear lumber like that out of your shipments. It is true, of course, that some manufacturers are robbers. They are too exacting and expect more of a mill than can be furnished, but they are the exception. The majority of the consuming trade takes a whole lot of lumber it knows is wrong rather than to make a kick about it, and when the millman clamors that he is being robbed it simply signifies in most cases that he has not put up the grade. The same waste and carelessness which have characterized all of his previous operations follow in his shipments and what he does not lose in wasteful manufacture he loses in kicks and bad accounts and has himself alone to blame.

The pine man who produces a little hardwood and the small operator who does not have sufficient stock to separate his grades and ship as desired by the consumer must sell his stock to the wholesale and yard trade, and he must meet the following conditions:

The yard man has to have properly manufactured lumber, good widths, lengths, thicknesses etc. and a high grade that he can rehandle thru his yard and separate into specialties for certain trade that he has developed. He therefore demands from the millman the very best and has to be technical and hold the millman up to the line, in order to come out whole himself.

The wholesaler who ships direct from the mill to the factory has been to the factory and knows what it wants. He has told it he will ship it what it wants. He therefore has to be as particular as the yard man about what he gets because he wants to keep his trade and wants to avoid kicks, so that whether his man goes to the mill to take up the stock or whether it is shipped and guaranteed he must have a good grade or his profit is consumed in the trouble he has over the car and the loss of trade.

The Burden Rests Upon the Millman

It can be seen therefore that whether the sale is made to the consumer, the yard, or the wholesaler, the ultimate destination is the consumer and if the yard man and the wholesaler give him the grade in order to keep his business the mill must give the same grade either to him or to them. Thus the man who produces any lumber, whether a small or a large quantity, ought to know the grade of it or have some one about the place who does know the grade of it, not merely think they know, and he would then know what is expected of him. Any wholesaler and any yard man would rather buy lumber from firms who know the grades and are willing to deliver them than from firms who do not, because they do not like to have continually to be correcting invoices and making deductions and have the millmen think they are being robbed when they are not. The burden of the whole matter therefore rests upon the millman. Before he can be a salesman he should know what he is selling. Many millmen figure they have a block, say, of 100,000 feet of 4/4 poplar. They think it should average them $21. They can not get anybody to buy it log run at $21, so it is finally sold on grade at prices the wholesaler knows are really a little too high but which he has to accept because he needs the stock. He orders it shipped and gives the millman a straight National grade on it, or whatever grade is agreed upon. The stock averages $16 and ships out about 90,000 feet. The millman may not say much but he privately thinks he has been robbed a little if not a whole lot. My contention is that if he knew what he was doing he would not have to think that. The wholesaler would much prefer to buy the lumber from a mill that was able to ship it and guarantee it, and then both would know that they had received a square deal.

To sell his lumber right, therefore, if he has not enough to ship out in straight carload lots, the millman should work the wholesale and yard trade but should understand that they have to have good lumber in order to do business and that he, the millman, should first produce good lumber; second, know his grades and what they are worth; third, get the price and give the grade. There is a difference of $3 to $5 a thousand in the grade of 4/4 No. 1 common oak shipped by Mr. Brown and that shipped by Mr. Smith. Mr. Smith gets more for his lumber not because he is a better salesman than Mr. Brown but because he is a better inspector and millman. He holds his lumber until it is dry. If the order calls for 15,000 feet, one-half or better and 14 and 16 feet long, he loads it that way and gives his customer just a little better grade than he is loking for. The result is the customer sends him another order at the same price. Two-thirds the salesmanship in selling lumber consists of putting up the grade. The best salesman can not sell the output of a mill that does not ship the grade. No salesman at all is required to sell the output of the mill that pleases the customer consistently.

Selling the output to a wholesaler by contract for an advance is all right where necessity requires it but as a rule there is no money made in that kind of a deal. It would work all right if business was always good but two-thirds of the time it is not good. The wholesaler has to buy the lumber low in cases of this kind to take care of market fluctuations; to take care of his credit risks, kicks etc., interest on his advances and insurance on the stock. He can make only about three-quarters the money value in advances so as to leave sufficient margin to take care of depreciation in grade and shrinkage in measure. Thus the millman who depends entirely upon this advance to run his plant finds it hard to meet all his payments. He runs behind and goes after the wholesaler for more money and they finally fall out. The only successful advance deals are where the mills have some capital, but not all they want, to carry the stock they should, and they therefore sell their output or a certain quantity to a wholesaler, receiving a 50 or 75 percent advance, and having sufficient capital or standing easily to finance themselves with this assistance. But I have seen many small millmen build a mill and finish owing for about half of it, having secured their timber the same way. They then make a contract with a wholesaler, selling him their output at starvation prices for monthly advances and hope out of these advances to meet their pay-rolls, their payments on mill and timber, and to make a little besides. They simply can not do it. The wholesaler should know they can not do it and not make contracts which his best judgment tells

him can not be met. If a list of these wholesale contracts were compiled covering the last five years I believe 90 percent of them would be shown up as having been unsatisfactory and unsuccessful. Hence, selling lumber by this method is not profitable for the mill and has frequently proved a disastrous one for the wholesaler.

The legitimate wholesaler is the best customer and the logical one for the small millman for several reasons. The most important is that the millman wants his money right away. The wholesaler will pay him at once and the consumer or yard man will not pay him until he gets the stock, and will then sometimes take his own sweet time about it. A number of mills want the matter of inspection settled at the mill. The wholesaler will arrange to settle it there and in other ways to accommodate the millman in a manner that the consumer or yard man will not. These things made the wholesaler in the lumber business a necessity and the talk about eliminating him is nothing but talk. The consumer and manufacturer like to get together and it is well for them to do so. Many of them do, but for the reasons stated a large proportion can not get together because of the way each conducts his business, and neither will change for the accommodation of the other. The wholesaler makes it his business to accommodate them both and thus finds his place in the scheme of things.

The wholesaler is generally the best credit risk for the millman. Many millmen are careless about their credits and in their anxiety to keep their stock moving they will take orders on which they know the credit is risky. Many of them do not use rating books at all, selling simply on the strength of their acquaintance with their buyers. Much of this risk is obviated in selling the wholesale trade by requiring the cash from it, thus eliminating the credit risk.

The way to make real money out of the sawmill business is to run the mill along scientific lines. Grade the lumber. Carry it until it is thoroly dry. Put up high grades and get the best market prices, selling either to the wholesaler or to the factory, but be fastidious about the character and number of your customers. Some observations on selling are the following:

Two-thirds of salesmanship is in putting up the grade.

Sell only rated trade. You will have trouble enough when selling the good ones. It is courting failure to take flyers on the others.

Fill ordess like they read and ship them at the time requested.

When your old customers hold up shipments in time of depression do not go out seeking new trade, because it is risky to sell a man in depressed times that would not give you an order when they were good.

Make the goods sell the goods.

Do not figure on luck. The only luck on which to figure is bad luck; then if it comes bad you are prepared for it; if it comes good you are that much better off.